Tactical Nuclear Weapons

Time for Control

Taina Susiluoto

Manas Publications
New Delhi - 110 002 (India)

MANAS PUBLICATIONS
(Publishers, Distributors, Importers & Exporters)
4402/5-A, Ansari Road (Opp. HDFC Bank)
Darya Ganj, New Delhi - 110 002 (India)
Phones: Off.: 011-23260783, 23265523,
Res.: 011-23842660
E-mail: manaspublications@gmail.com
www.manaspublications.in

1st Edn

ISBN: 978-81-7049-213-9 (13 Digits)
81-7049-213-0 (10 Digits)

Rs. 495/-

Designed at
Manas Publications
Printed in India at
HS Offset Printers, Delhi
and published by Mrs Suman Lata for
Manas Publications, 4402/5-A,
Ansari Road (Opp HDFC Bank),
Darya Ganj, New Delhi - 110002 (INDIA)

CONTENTS

PREFACE

To mark the tenth anniversary of the 1991 Bush-Gorbachev unilateral declarations on tactical nuclear weapons, UNIDIR and its collaborating partners held a meeting in September 2001 at the United Nations in New York. The meeting took place days after the terrible attacks against the World Trade Center and the Pentagon on the 11th September.

At the UNIDIR meeting and many times since that fateful day, the issue of terrorist attacks using weapons of mass destruction and, in particular, fissile materials has been raised. The continuing lack of control over tactical nuclear weapons means that there is a clear and present danger that tactical nuclear weapons may have been, or may be in the future, stolen or sold to those with an intent to use them for the purposes of terrorism.

Tactical nuclear weapons are a particularly dangerous category of nuclear weapons. They are portable, often integrated into conventional force structures and, in some cases, less well guarded than their strategic counterparts. Despite the 1991 Presidential Nuclear Initiatives, there has never been any formal agreement on the removal and elimination of tactical nuclear weapons. Despite periodic updates on progress, data were never agreed, only proportions of numbers to be eliminated or stored were declared. Still today a great deal of uncertainty exists over the implementation of the 1991 unilateral declarations.

Perhaps more worrying, there seems to be a renewed interest in this category of nuclear weapons. Post September 11, in addition to the concerns over the terrorist use of nuclear weapons and nuclear materials, there have been discussions and debates, in public and in private, on the potential use by States of small, low yield nuclear weapons to attack underground hideouts of terrorist leaders or terrorists' weapons manufacturing facilities. In addition the use of nuclear weapons as a response to chemical and biological weapons attacks is also being debated. None of these debates has led to official policy changes, but with the increasing concerns over the long-term adherence to the comprehensive nuclear test ban treaty, it is not beyond the realm of possibility that new small, short-range and "useable" nuclear weapons could be on the horizon.

In response to these developments, and with the support of the United Nations Secretary General's Advisory Board on Disarmament Matters, UNIDIR continued a study began in 1999 on the situation regarding tactical nuclear weapons. UNIDIR hosted a first workshop in Geneva in March 2000 at which papers analysing such issues as the current situation, numbers and definitions, and regional approaches were presented. In September 2001 the second workshop in New York, looked at issues of transparency, verification, control, legislation, terrorism, potential development of TNWs and the link to concerns over nuclear testing.

There is sustained and increasing interest over these aspects of tactical nuclear weapons. It is indeed time to control this class of weapons. Perhaps it may already be too late to prevent these weapons getting into the hands of those with the intent to use them or the materials contained therein, so as to cause injury and mayhem to targeted civilian populations. But we must start from here and at least bring under control those weapons that are covered by the 1991 Initiatives. Ten years is late enough. Let's hope that it is not too late.

This volume is a collection of the papers that were presented at the New York seminar. Not all the papers presented in New York have been published in this volume and some of the papers have been updated to take account of political developments. A collection of some of these papers was circulated in draft form at the 2002 Preparatory Committee for the 2005 Review Conference of the Non-Proliferation Treaty.

UNIDIR's collaborating partners for this meeting were the Monterey Institute Center for Nonproliferation Studies, the Peace Research Institute Frankfurt, Green Cross International and Global Green USA. Many thanks go to them for their support and practical contributions throughout the planning and execution of this project.

Sincere gratitude goes to the generosity of our financial sponsors for the meeting and the publication the Governments of Finland, Norway, the Netherlands, Germany and New Zealand.

I should particularly like to thank the authors of the papers: President Mikhail Gorbachev, the former President of the USSR, William C. Potter and Nikolai Sokov of the Center for Nonproliferation Studies, Monterey Institute of International Studies, Rose Gottemoeller of the Carnegie

Endowment for International Peace, Pavel Podvig of the Moscow Institute of Physics and Technology, Alistair Miller of the Fourth Freedom Forum, Frank von Hippel and Josh Handler of Princeton University, Alexander Pikayev of the Carnegie Endowment in Moscow, Jack Spencer of the Heritage Foundation, Taina Susiluoto of UNIDIR, Sergey Radchenko of UNIDIR and the London School of Economics, Rebecca Johnson of the Acronym Institute, Ambassador Miguel Marin Bosch of the Government of Mexico and Charles Mead of RAND.

Thanks also to Terence Taylor of the International Institute of Strategic Studies and Robert Nelson of Princeton University for the presentations they made at the conference, despite great difficulties.

Most of all, it must be said that the meeting and the publication would never have taken place without the unfailing efforts of Taina Susiluoto and her team at UNIDIR. Taina worked with Nicolas Florquin on loan from the Monterey Institute and the Department for Disarmament Affairs and Sergey Radchenko from the London School of Economics in the planning of the meeting and collection of the papers. Isabelle Roger and Jackie Seck provided administrative support; the publication was edited by Steve Tulliu and brought to press by Anita Blétry.

I am very grateful for all the hard work and support that went into this work. Now, however, the hard work must not go to waste and urgent political and practical action needs to be taken to control tactical nuclear weapons.

Patricia Lewis
Director
UNIDIR
Geneva

STATEMENT BY FORMER PRESIDENT MIKHAIL GORBACHEV[1]

Dear friends,

I am sorry I could not join you today for this important gathering to discuss the 10th anniversary of the reciprocal unilateral commitments announced by former President George Bush and myself in October 1991. Together these commitments amount to one of the deepest and most comprehensive programmes of nuclear weapons reduction the world has ever seen. I congratulate the organizers of this important event and welcome the delegates, including representatives of many nations.

You are meeting soon after the horrific tragedy of the recent terrorist attacks on the United States. My first reaction to it was to send a cable to President Bush, expressing my profound condolences and feelings of solidarity with the American people. The terrible crime was committed not only against America but against all humankind, which is now facing an unprecedented challenge. It is only by common efforts that we will be able to find a response to it.

We need a thoughtful analysis of problems like the root causes of violence, fanaticism and terrorism, and a strategy for dealing with them. This strategy must be responsible, wise and effective.

The tragedy of September 11 was a heart-breaking reminder of the fragility of life and civilisation. Like Chernobyl, it should make us think hard about the dangers posed by weapons of mass destruction.

The detonation of just one nuclear warhead equals the impact of 100 Chernobyl explosions. During this time of crisis and uncertainty, we must

1 Letter from President Mikhail Gorbachev, former President of the Soviet Union, to the participants to the UNIDIR workshop "Time to Control Tactical Nuclear Weapons", held at United Nations Headquarters in New York, USA, on 24 September 2001, to mark the occasion of the 10th anniversary of the issuing of the 1991 Presidential Nuclear Initiatives.

work together in reducing this ultimate danger. I therefore salute and encourage your efforts to control the threat of tactical nuclear weapons, too many of which are still intact ten years after the end of the Cold War.

Indeed, one of my greatest regrets and concerns is that the decade of the 1990s was not used effectively to do away with the political, military and environmental legacies of the Cold War. The opportunities opened up by the end of that decades-long confrontation were missed; too often, the inertia of Cold War thinking defined the actions of our political leaders. Not nearly enough was done to redirect the resources of the world's leading powers to tasks such as bridging the gap between rich and poor nations, healing the environment and combating terrorism.

The time has come to relegate to the past the Cold War mindset and to dismantle the dangerous apparatus that it created. Let us remember that the United States and Russia are under the obligation they assumed by signing the Nuclear Non-Proliferation Treaty, to eventually eliminate and abolish all nuclear weapons. The recent Non-Proliferation Treaty review conference called for "further reduction of non-strategic nuclear weapons, based on unilateral initiatives and as an integral part of the nuclear arms reduction and disarmament process".

I attach equal importance to unilateral arms reduction commitments and to bilateral and multilateral disarmament treaties. It would be a cause of great concern if major nuclear powers abandoned or neglected multilateral forums, or took steps that would endanger the entire structure of arms control treaties, many of which, such as the 1972 ABM Treaty, are of as much value today as they were during the decades of nuclear confrontation. By all means nuclear powers should display special responsibility setting an example for the rest of the world and avoiding any steps that might lead to weapons of mass destruction proliferation.

In my role as President of Green Cross International, I have continued to build upon the work we began with the INF and START Treaties, the Chemical Weapons Convention and the 1991 unilateral commitments of the United States and Russia. Our organization has been a key actor in the United States and Russia to eliminate the threat of chemical weapons, to build new coalitions to facilitate their environmentally safe destruction, and help encourage public engagement in the disarmament process. Similarly, we have worked to help Russia safely destroy strategic motors from the missiles that once carried nuclear warheads. Now, we are expanding our work with reducing the threat of nuclear weapons and exploring how we can assist in eliminating biological weapons as well.

You will be able to learn more about the activities and thinking of the Green Cross on issues that are directly relevant to the subject of your conference, such as de-alerting strategic nuclear weapons and reducing the threat of proliferation, theft or accidental use of tactical nuclear weapons from the report of the Global Green USA, the United States branch of Green Cross International, presented to you. I urge you to give careful consideration to these ideas and suggestions.

It is entirely fitting that you are meeting at the United Nations, an organization that will have to play a much greater role if we are to deal successfully with the multiple threats and challenges we are facing in the new century. I salute your determination to persevere in the cause of disarmament and wish you success in the day ahead. Together, I know we can succeed.

Mikhail Gorbachev

WORKSHOP REPORT

Ten years ago Presidents George Bush and Mikhail Gorbachev issued directions to begin one of the deepest and most comprehensive programmes of nuclear weapons reduction the world has yet seen.

These reciprocal unilateral Declarations still constitute the only regime covering tactical nuclear weapons (TNWs). At the same time, however, these Declarations suffer from inherent difficulties and weaknesses that metigate their impact. The seminar focused on further efforts needed from the international community to strengthen and improve the workings of the Declarations.

The seminar brought together government officials and diplomats dealing with arms control and disarmament matters as well as selected nongovernmental experts specialised in tactical nuclear weapons. It is a part of a long-term project launched by UNIDIR in order to support efforts to address and curb the problem of TNWs.

The seminar was held off the record and therefore all comments made by participants during the meeting are not directly attributed. This report reflects the substance of the lively discussions held, and of the recommendations suggested.

THE 1991 DECLARATIONS AND THE EVOLVING SECURITY FRAMEWORK

The Utility of Unilateral Initiatives

Unilateral measures are instruments that may be used to enhance the process of arms control. The beneficial effects of unilateral arms control initiatives are weighted against their inherent uncertainties and weaknesses, particularly with respect to their implementation. In the light of growing reliance on unilateral measures, specific attention has to be devoted to these issues from the perspectives of international law and politics.

Although unilateral measures may be an effective means to bring about quick solutions they also often fail to satisfy in the long term. As a result, unilateral regimes may need to be strengthened along the way with different measures and hopefully even be codified into a contractual framework.

Legally binding arms control instruments contribute to the stability of the international security system, and are particularly important at a time when the "the crisis of arms control and multilateralism" is becoming commonly acknowledged. The flaws of the existing arms control treaties, particularly reflecting the past adversarial relationship, have to be acknowledged. There is a need to move towards a new structure of a formal strategic framework.

The 1991 Parallel Unilateral Declaration

With respect to the 1991 initiatives, ten years ago, at the time of the breakup of the Soviet Union, the United States and the USSR shared grave concerns about the status and high level of operational readiness of tactical nuclear weapons. By mandating the withdrawal of warheads to central storage facilities and the destruction of some of them, the Unilateral Declarations were effective in quickly addressing these issues, but only partially because important questions regarding the implementation and monitoring of the announced provisions remained unresolved.

There is a strong need for more certainty, predictability and transparency in the implementation of the 1991 unilateral Declarations. In this respect, the recent controversial media reports of the possible deployment of tactical nuclear weapons in Kaliningrad by Russia are a pertinent example. The likely enlargement of NATO raises fears in some quarters in Moscow of Kaliningrad becoming an isolated island surrounded by a powerful military alliance. Deployment of tactical nuclear weapons for the defense of the enclave is sometimes touted as an option. Such a development, however, would cast serious doubt on the continued viability of the Bush/Gorbachev declarations. One possible remedy identified for precluding this scenario would be providing information on Russia's stockpiles of TNWs in exchange for a binding obligation by NATO not to deploy tactical nuclear weapons on the territories of new member States.

Another example concerns the notion of "central storage facilities" in the context of removing warheads from naval platforms and storing them. In the United States, the term central storage means "geographically-central storage" while in the Russian case, the phrase refers to central storage at naval bases. Russian, it seems, prefers to keep weapons close at hand. In this respect there are as yet no agreed definitions, concepts or modalities of implementation and monitoring regarding the control of tactical nuclear weapons.

Strengthening the Current TNW Regime within the Context of the Current Arms Control Dialogue

The current political situation does not seem to lend itself to the negotiation of a legally binding instrument on TNWs. Instead, different transparency and confidence-building measures could be grafted onto the 1991 regime or additional measures could be evolved to push for the further reduction of TNWs.

The United States and the Russian Federation are presently in the process of hammering out a new strategic framework, to be premised on openness, mutual confidence, and significant opportunities for cooperation. Particularly, the two States have indicated that this will include a substantial reduction of offensive nuclear forces.

In this respect, it is unclear whether these discussions include the goals outlined in the 1997 Helsinki Agreement that called for transparency in the reduction of tactical nuclear weapons. There is concern over the danger that the issue of TNWs might be dropped from the discussions. It would be strongly desirable, particularly from the point of view of European security, to include tactical nuclear weapons in the planned reductions as well as develop new transparency and confidence-building measures related to this category of weapons.

To pave the way for fresh negotiations on TNWs, we propose a set of measures to strengthen the 1991 TNWs control regime. One of the identified priority measures would be the reaffirmation of the 1991 Declarations and the introduction of regular information exchange as well as common guidelines for the implementation of the Declarations. Any of these measures could be introduced as a Memorandum of Understanding or other suitable international instrument between the United States and Russia.

NEW NUCLEAR WEAPONS DEVELOPMENT AND TESTING

Dangerous Desire for "Mini-Nukes"

There is a growing interest in the development of new nuclear weapons and concerns about the impact that this would have on the nuclear weapons test ban regime. Some prominent advisers in the United States Government who favour a military role for TNWs, now advocate the testing and development of new, smaller, more readily usable nuclear warheads and weapons systems for eventual deployment.

However, the evolving new strategic nuclear framework needs to be responsive to terrorist threats. One of the latest envisaged scenarios is the utilisation of "mini-nukes" for the neutralisation of hardened missile silos and command bunkers of terrorist organizations or "rogue" governments. There are worries about the impact that the 11 September attacks could have on the emerging strategic framework and particularly on the role of nuclear weapons in crisis situations.

Earth Penetrating Weapons

Earth penetrating nuclear weapons amplify the effect of seismic shocks, which may destroy buried hardened targets. It is estimated that an Earth-penetrating weapon equipped with a nuclear warhead whose yield is only one ton would still produce highly radioactive debris and cause tens of thousands of casualties.

Currently, much discussion centers around whether such new tactical nuclear weapons would have to be tested in order to determine their efficacy. Many are concerned that developing such weapons would involve testing, which in turn would run counter to the objective of the Comprehensive Test Ban Treaty (CTBT) that the United States has signed but not ratified. Some statements from the American nuclear weapons laboratories, however, indicate that testing would not necessarily be required for the development of new, smaller TNWs.

Implications for the CTBT

Plans to develop new kinds of tactical nuclear weapons further burden the already aching Comprehensive Test Ban Treaty. The CTBT is a basic force in the prevention of the spread of nuclear weapons. Some participants felt that tampering with the CTBT could well open a Pandora's Box of nuclear proliferation. At the same time it is acknowledged that the CTBT has faults, such as for instance the provisions regarding its entry into force. Ultimately, however, taking into account the importance of the CTBT, it is vital to respect and abide by its provisions regardless of whether or not the treaty is actually in force.

TNWs AND TERRORISM

In the wake of the 11 September terrorist attacks against the World Trade Centre in New York and the Pentagon, the UNIDIR seminar was the first event of its kind for which non-member organizations were allowed entry to the United Nations Headquarters. Due to the exceptional circumstances a special Roundtable discussion on tactical nuclear weapons and terrorism was scheduled. The exchange of views was vivid and the participants found the discussion timely.

Deliberations focused on three main topics: 1) the threat of the use of nuclear weapons by terrorists; 2) the use of nuclear weapons against terrorists; and 3) regional security considerations in South Asia.

Threat of TNW Terrorism

Threat of Terrorists Possessing "Loose Nukes"

The 11 September attacks have brought attention to the possibility that terrorists might deliberately seek to inflict mass casualties as an objective. The ability to use weapons of mass destruction, particularly nuclear weapons, as instruments of terror is largely a function of their access to such weapons. It is said, for instance, that groups such as Al-Qaeda have in the past expressed interest in acquiring weapons of mass destruction capabilities.

Nuclear weapons possessor countries generally devote considerable effort to protecting this part of their arsenal. Therefore, stealing tactical nuclear weapons should be a difficult task. In this respect chemical or biological weapons might pose a greater danger.

The trouble with tactical nuclear weapons, however, is that these weapons exist in greater numbers than any other types of nuclear weapons, they are not governed by contractual instruments and that their quantity poses a real risk. For instance, in the past, occasional reports have surfaced that since the dissolution of the Soviet Union not all former Soviet tactical nuclear weapons have been properly accounted for. Verifying this claim of "loose nukes" is naturally difficult. Other potential sources of risk derive from the modalities of how these weapons are stored and the lack of exact knowledge of where they are located and of how they are deployed. In particular, concerns are raised over tactical nuclear weapons deployed in the form of aircraft munitions and short-range missile warheads.

Complete tactical nuclear weapons systems are still difficult to use without key information and technical components. However, theft of TNW components and their means of delivery should be taken seriously when thinking about the security challenges involved in protecting TNWs.

Threat of Terrorists Attempting to Build Radiological Weapons

The United States and Russia are currently engaged in a major programme designed to ensure the protection of fissile materials. Bilateral projects have also successfully converted many Russian nuclear weapons scientists into civilian professions. The beneficial effects of these programmes, particularly due to the recent events, should be expanded and strengthened.

The process needed for the delivery of a small nuclear weapon could be beyond the capabilities of most terrorist groups. Terrorists might be tempted to acquire nuclear material with the objective of exploding a radiological weapon. By mixing radioactive material with conventional high explosives, a terrorist group might be able to spread deadly radiological contamination over a wide area and cause severe and lasting disruption.

Tight control over nuclear-weapon-usable fissile materials, including export controls, is immediately needed. In order to ensure that this material does not end up in the wrong hands, measures such as installing radiation scanners at key facilities—ports and border crossings—as well as tightening physical security at nuclear labs, powerplants or naval depots to prevent the theft of fissile materials, could significantly improve the situation.

Nuclear Option Against Terrorists

An article entitled *"Time to Use the Nuclear Option"* published in the Washington Times 14 September 2001, just days prior to the seminar, argued that tactical nuclear weapons should be used to eliminate Osama Bin Laden and his supporters.

Most participants at the meeting, however, ruled out the possibility that the United States would use nuclear weapons and thereby break the 55 years old nuclear non-use taboo as well as face the severe likely political consequences. However, there has been much debate in recent years as to whether using nuclear weapons would be a legitimate response to a BW attack.

Regional Security Considerations in South Asia

The possibility of regional tension expanding in South Asia due to the American military campaign against terrorist groups based in Afghanistan raised concerns over the security of Pakistan's nuclear materials, particularly in regard to stability of an unelected military government.

The importance of custodial safeguards for nuclear weapons as well as materials can not be stressed enough. Preventive measures could include: 1) the enhancement of nuclear materials protection and accounting methods to strengthen storage of these materials; and 2) the removal of fissile material to the United States following the past examples of the bilateral Russian-US programs.

CONCLUSION

Emphasizing the vital importance of strengthening the 1991 tactical nuclear weapons regime the participants in the seminar put forth a number of recommendations, a summary of which is presented below. In addition, the participants affirmed the desirability of including tactical nuclear weapons as part of any further reductions of offensive nuclear forces, currently considered under the new strategic framework discussed by the Russian Federation and United States of America.

SUMMARY OF RECOMMENDATIONS

Strengthening the 1991 Regime on Tactical Nuclear Weapons

1. The United States of America and the Russian Federation could:

- reaffirm the 1991 Declarations;
- exchange information on the implementation of the 1991 Declarations;
- adopt mutually agreed guidelines for the implementation of the 1991 Declarations;
- introduce transparency measures on stocks by category (deployed, long-term storage, slated for elimination) and distribution by region;
- expand the Cooperative Threat Reduction (CTR) program to include the protection and dismantlement of TNWs;
- identify specific categories of weapons to which transparency measures could be applied, e.g. SLCM (sea-launched cruise missiles).

2. Increase the funding of the US Cooperative Threat Reduction Programme by encouraging the participation of other States;

3. Increase transparency with regards to stockpiles of TNWs in all nuclear weapon States and States possessing nuclear weapons;

4. Include tactical nuclear weapons in the planned unilateral reductions of offensive nuclear forces by the Russian Federation and the United States of America.

5. A binding obligation by NATO not to deploy tactical nuclear weapons on the territories of new member States;

6. Commitments by all nuclear-weapon States to withdraw and repatriate their tactical nuclear weapons to national territories;

7. Adopt appropriate verification measures to monitor adequately the control of tactical nuclear weapons.

New Nuclear Weapons Development and Testing

1. Reduce the military role attributed to TNWs, and withdraw any current plans to develop new nuclear weapons or resume testing;

2. Respect and abide by the CTBT regardless of whether or not the treaty is actually in force.

TNWs and Terrorism

1. An understanding that in combating terrorism concerned states will not resort to the use or threat of use of nuclear weapons;

2. Increase security in order to guarantee the safety of nuclear weapons, their components and delivery systems, as well as of nuclear materials and facilities;

3. Further reduce stockpiles of tactical nuclear weapons in order to lower the risk emanating from the existing large numbers of TNWs;

4. Increase the capacity to fully account for all tactical nuclear weapons and materials in relevant States.

PART I

The 1991 Declaration and the Evolving Security Framework

CHAPTER 1

ADVANTAGES AND DISADVANTAGES OF UNILATERAL ARMS CONTROL POLICY

Rose Gottemoeller

Unilateral action in the arms control arena can have beneficial effects, especially by accelerating reductions. This "accelerator effect" was in fact one of the core rationales for the 1991/92 Presidential Nuclear Initiatives: they enabled tactical or non-strategic nuclear weapons to be removed quickly from a status of operational readiness. Thus, at a time of crisis, when the Soviet Union was breaking apart rapidly, these unilateral initiatives conducted in parallel between the United States and Russia addressed wide-ranging concerns about accidental or unauthorized use of these weapons.

The beneficial effects of unilateral actions are not unvarnished, however. Difficulties come in the implementation of unilateral arms reductions, because there is no agreement about how they will be conducted, or indeed about what will be included in the reduction process. In the implementation of the 1991/92 declarations, for example, Russia and the United States ended up with two quite different approaches to the reductions. For budgetary reasons, the United States ceased training and operational activities to support non-strategic nuclear warheads on the vast majority of its naval surface platforms once the weapons had been removed from deployment.

Russia, in contrast, continued to train and conduct operational activities even after the weapons were removed. According to Russian naval officers, unless there is a legally-binding arms control agreement, Russian law and naval procedure forbids them from changing their practices—in other words, the ships continue to operate as if nuclear weapons were aboard, and are certified as nuclear-capable. Without agreed methods of implementation for the reductions, the Russians are not required to change their ways. However, without monitoring and inspection procedures, outsiders find it difficult to determine that the weapons have been removed.

Another difficulty is in the lack of agreed definitions. Under the 1991/92 declarations, for example, the two countries agreed to remove the weapons to "central storage facilities", a term that was not further defined in the discussions. The United States removed the weapons to geographically central storage facilities, while the Russian Federation removed them to central storage facilities at the naval bases where the ships that normally deploy them are based. According to a Russian naval officer, the weapons are off their deployment platforms, but are kept "close at hand".

These differences in how the two countries implemented the 1991/92 declarations may account in part for the problems that were encountered in early 2001, when the Russians were accused of re-introducing nuclear warheads into their military enclave at Kaliningrad. The weaknesses in the declarations were highlighted when the Poles, neighbours to Kaliningrad, demanded an inspection to determine whether or not nuclear weapons were present on their borders. The response of the United States Department of State was to note that "We do not inspect except as pursuant to an arms control agreement".[1]

In addition to problems for neighbours, unilateral reductions also impose a large burden on the threat assessors and military planners of each country who are required to accurately assess the threat and define the necessary response in the interest of their country's national security. If the implementation of the measures is uncertain and there are no agreed measures for monitoring their execution, threat assessors and military planners are placed in a difficult position. They must call what they see, which may be a greater capability than actually exists in the military forces of the other party.

The net effect is likely to be that planning for a response against the threat will continue at a higher level than would have been the case with a verifiable arms control agreement. The two parties, in other words, do not achieve the same diminution of military threat that they would have attained had they agreed to monitored implementation. They must, in that case, continue to bear the expense of a full-scale response.

Resolving this tension between the beneficial aspects of unilateral reductions and the need for more surety in implementation is possible. However, this process involves circling back to negotiated regimes. There are two ways to go about it—either building on the foundation of existing regimes, or developing additional negotiated measures. An example of the first approach would be to use the Strategic Arms Reductions Treaty (START) I Verification Protocol as the mechanism for implementing further strategic force reductions. It would be the foundation on which to build further unilateral reductions. In fact, this appears to be the approach currently favoured by the United States and Russia to achieve strategic reductions.

An example of the second approach is the Verification and Monitoring Protocol of the Biological and Toxin Weapons Convention (BTWC). Although the current version of this Protocol has come under attack by the Bush administration, the concept remains intact: the BWC has been in place for some time, but has lacked a legally binding verification regime. Currently, although with difficulty, the parties to the Convention are negotiating to provide for monitoring and verification, or at a minimum transparency, into implementation of the regime.

A third approach, which may be productive in the case of tactical nuclear weapons (TNWs), would be to begin not from the foundation of a negotiated regime, but with a "pilot project" to develop monitoring and transparency concepts. In this case, Russia and the United States might refer to the 1997 Helsinki Statement, wherein the two countries agreed to explore new measures for monitoring non-strategic nuclear weapons and sea-launched cruise missiles.

Traditionally, these systems have been the most difficult to monitor and verify, because of their small size and the variation in their configuration—i.e., the same delivery platforms can accommodate both nuclear and conventional munitions. Advances in sensor technologies, including information barriers, and the potential for greater access to deployment platforms, may make monitoring and verification of the status of such weapons more feasible than it has been in the past. This potential could be explored through a "pilot project" to examine the application of some of these new technologies in operational settings. At a minimum, such a pilot approach would contribute to enhance confidence regarding the declarations. At a maximum, it would provide the first step toward a more predictable and perhaps legally binding regime for TNWs.

In sum, there are reasons to be optimistic that more attention can be gained for the problem of controlling non-strategic nuclear weapons. This optimism originates in technological developments, but also in the possibility that an overall improvement in the relationship between Russia and the United States will enable more joint presence and interaction on operational platforms. A step-by-step or pilot project approach would probably work best to launch the process, however, rather than early insistence on negotiating a complete regime.

Endnotes

1. Quoted in "Russia Places Tactical Nukes in Kaliningrad, Worries NATO", Editorial Information Network, 8 January 2001.

CHAPTER 2

AN UPDATE ON EFFORTS TO REDUCE TACTICAL NUCLEAR WEAPONS*

William C. Potter

THE CURRENT PREDICAMENT

Ironically, at a time when the Bush administration appears increasingly enthusiastic about unilateral approaches to nuclear arms control, it has been noticeably silent about the informal arms control regime on tactical nuclear weapons (TNWs) created ten years ago on the basis of parallel, unilateral declarations made by George Bush and Mikhail Gorbachev. As a disarmament measure, these unilateral declarations have resulted in the elimination of more nuclear charges than all the negotiated agreements between the United States and the Soviet Union/Russia, and also have led to the redeployment in central storage of thousands of additional weapons.

Notwithstanding the significant accomplishments of the 1991/92 declarations, the informal regime suffers from a number of serious deficiencies:

- Unilateral statements are not legally binding. They can be disavowed without prior notification;
- The parallel, unilateral declarations do not provide a mechanism for their mutual modification;
- The 1991/92 informal regime does not provide for data exchange or any verification and transparency measures. It, therefore, is impossible to have confidence in the implementation of the declarations and to ascertain the status of the remaining TNWs. Russia, for example, has not provided any new information on its implementation of the 1991 declarations, since its statement at the 2000 NPT Review Conference;

- Reductions under the unilateral statements were conceived in terms of the percentage of the arsenal rather than with respect to agreed ceilings. No reference was made to the total number of TNWs at the time of the statements and there is no indication of the numbers to be reduced. Neither the United States nor Russia has released official public information regarding the number or location of their TNWs, including their central storage sites (as was highlighted by the controversy about possible Russian redeployments of TNWs in Kaliningrad).

Because of these shortcomings, the existing informal regime is poorly equipped to withstand increasing challenges, such as the growing scepticism in both countries about the role of arms control treaties and agreements in providing for their national security; the revival of interest in TNWs in Russia and the United States; and growing pressure in Russia to redeploy, remanufacture and/or modernise its TNWs force as existing stocks near the end of their service life.

There has been a tendency in the United States—particularly by senior members of the present administration—to discount the deficiencies of the current informal TNWs regime, to minimise the likelihood of its erosion, and to dismiss the threat to United States national security posed by Russian TNWs. These assumptions are sorely mistaken for reasons that have been elaborated in a number of other publications.[1] Here it is sufficient to note that significant dangers exist for the United States and other nations due to both the physical properties of TNWs and the policies for their deployment and employment. These threats relate to:

- the vulnerability of TNW to theft and unauthorised use;
- forward basing;
- pre-delegation of launch authority;
- trends in modernisation;
- attractiveness to potential proliferators, including non-State actors; and
- inadequate physical protection (especially for TNWs designated for aircraft missions because these weapons are not kept at central storage sites in Russia).

RECENT DEVELOPMENTS

Given these problems, what positive and negative developments have transpired in the past 18 months relevant to TNWs control?

One of the few positive occurrences is language in the Final Document of the 2000 Non-Proliferation Treaty (NPT) Review Conference, which for the first time in Review Conference history includes agreed text regarding the reduction of non-strategic nuclear weapons. Although the language of the declaration was weakened substantially by Russia's insistence upon the clause "based on unilateral initiatives", the strong and broad support for further reductions evident at the 2000 Conference should make it easier in the future to utilise the review process to promote stronger language on TNWs reductions. That positive picture, however, is clouded somewhat by the fact that the Bush administration may find it hard to support implementation of the Final Document when the issue is revisited at next year's NPT PrepCom because of the document's inclusion of a number of objectionable items in the list of 13 "practical steps", of which TNWs reductions is one.

If there is some prospect for ongoing multilateral discussion of TNWs controls in the NPT context, the chances of United States-Russian negotiations is much less encouraging. Although shortly after the conclusion of the 2000 NPT Review Conference the United States formally proposed to Russia that both States reaffirm the 1991 parallel declarations, Russia chose not to respond directly to the proposal. Instead, it reiterated the position that the United States withdraw its TNWs from Europe. Today, with START III dead in the water, there appears to be no prospect in the near term for progress in addressing TNWs within the strategic arms control negotiating arena as once was envisaged. Although it may be possible to achieve future reductions of strategic nuclear arms on the basis of less formal negotiations, neither the Bush nor Putin administrations have shown any interest to date in the further reduction of TNWs or in the strengthening of the existing non-legally binding TNW regime Another promising means to control non-strategic nuclear weapons—the creation of a Nuclear-Weapons-Free Zone (NWFZ) in Central Asia—also has been stymied for over a year. The problem relates primarily to a shift in Russian diplomacy, which now interprets the Tashkent Treaty on Collective Security to allow for Russian deployment of nuclear weapons in Central Asia under certain circumstances. This policy shift has led a number of the Central Asian States to support language in the nearly complete draft NWFZ treaty, which, if adopted, could be interpreted as sanctioning the presence of TNWs in a NWFZ. Although it is hard to imagine the utility of TNWs in meeting security threats in Central Asia, the Russian resolve to keep all of its military options open has probably increased since the post-11 September rise in intensity of conflict in the region. The new prospect of a long term United States military presence in the area likely reinforces that conviction. The last noteworthy, recent development is the more frequent discussions in the United States and Russian press since 11 September 2001 of both the access of non-State actors to TNWs and the possible use of TNWs by State actors. Regarding the former issue, although there has been no fundamental change recently in the vulnerability of United States or Russian TNWs arsenals, the potential for diversion of weapons not in central storage is a risk that merits more attention.

Since spring 1999, following the North Atlantic Treaty Organisation (NATO) campaign against Yugoslavia, there have been serious discussions among relevant Russian military and foreign policy organs about the potential utility of TNWs as a means for both deterrence and conflict deescalation. United States policymakers also have begun to look more seriously at the role TNWs can play in a variety of scenarios ranging from deterrence, to political reassurance, to targeting of hardened chemical and biological weapons facilities. Although the rapid defeat of Taliban and Al-Qaeda forces removed pressure to consider the use of non-conventional weapons in Afghanistan, there were early indications that the Bush administration had not entirely ruled out employment of TNWs in its military response to the perpetrators of the terrorist attacks on the United States and their protectors. Secretary Rumsfeld, for example, very carefully chose not to exclude that possibility when pressed on the subject in a September 2001 television interview. Even more reckless calls for TNWs use appeared in the American media. In short, the so-called "respectable centre stage for debate" on the development, threat to use, and actual employment of TNWs appears to be expanding

NEXT STEPS

There are no easy or obvious solutions to the problems of TNWs arms control that readily meet the test of political feasibility. One can, however, identify a number of approaches that hold some promise, and that should be examined in more detail.

Reaffirmation of the 1991/92 Declarations

A very high priority should be given to identifying measures that reinforce the informal and fragile TNWs regime. Among the most important steps that could be taken in this regard is the reaffirmation by the United States and Russia in a joint statement of their continued commitment to the 1991/92 parallel unilateral declarations. It also would be highly desirable, but more difficult politically, to codify the existing declarations into a legally binding treaty.

Transparency Measures

A high priority also should be attached to exploring means to enhance TNWs transparency. Although it would be preferable to do so within the context of legally binding, negotiated accords, it probably is unrealistic to expect formal negotiations any time soon. How then might one proceed? One approach would be to rely upon largely unverifiable voluntary data exchanges, perhaps regarding the number of TNW stocks by category (i.e., deployed, reserve/long-term storage, slated for elimination), and their distribution by region. Another variant of this less formal approach is what Lewis Dunn has referred to as a "Mix and Match" strategy. It would reinforce the TNWs regime by selectively supporting a variety of related activities outside of the formal United States-Russian arms control negotiation arena.

Perhaps the best example of such an approach is to expand the activities of the Cooperative Threat Reduction (CTR) program to include the protection and dismantlement of TNWs. CTR funds currently are not designated to assist the safeguarding and dismantlement of TNWs in Russia, although that objective is not inconsistent with the objective of the original Nunn-Lugar program. Among the potential gains from the expansion of the CTR mandate would be the acceleration of the process of securing TNWs and their consolidation at fewer facilities, acceleration of the pace of TNWs dismantlement, greater likelihood of Russian receptivity to further arms reductions involving TNWs, increased transparency (a part of the CTR process) for TNWs dismantlement, and more safeguards for the fissile material by-products of the dismantlement process. Given the growing interest on the part of a number of countries in TNWs disarmament, it would be highly desirable for other States to join the United States in this expanded CTR effort.

Multilateral Fora

It also makes sense to reinforce the informal TNWs regime in multilateral fora, including the NPT review process and the United Nations General Assembly. In particular, one should build upon the consensus on further reductions of TNWs reflected in the Final Document of the 2000 NPT Review Process. It would be very appropriate, for example, for the First Committee to adopt a resolution on "Additional Measures to Reduce Non-Strategic Nuclear Weapons". Such a resolution might:

1. *Note* the particular responsibility of the nuclear-weapon States for accountable, transparent and verified reductions in nuclear weapons leading to nuclear disarmament;
2. *Call* upon the nuclear-weapon States to reduce non-strategic nuclear weapons with a view to their elimination as an integral part of nuclear arms reductions;
3. *Agree* on the importance of preserving and strengthening the 1991/1992 Presidential Nuclear Initiatives on non-strategic nuclear weapons;
4. *Call* for further confidence-building and transparency measures to reduce the threats posed by non-strategic nuclear weapons;
5. *Agree* that adoption of a framework on data exchanges covering non-strategic nuclear weapons and warhead deactivation would contribute to enhanced transparency; and
6. *Decide* to include in the provisional agenda of its fifty-seventh session the item entitled "Further Reductions and Transparency in Non-Strategic Nuclear Weapons", and to review the implementation of the present resolution at that session.

Mexico circulated a significant draft resolution on "Reductions of Non-Strategic Nuclear Weapons" at the opening of the 2001 meeting of the First Committee. However, it was unable to obtain support from several key States and chose not to submit a formal resolution. Instead, it made a useful but diluted statement without the strong support of the New Agenda Coalition (NAC). The only other delegation to address the issue at the First Committee was Finland, which made a weak statement on behalf of itself and Sweden about the importance of unilateral measures in the domain of TNWs.

A much more positive and assertive stance toward TNWs was taken by many States at the first session of the NPT Preparatory Committee, held in New York, 8-19 April 2002. A large number of delegations called for progress beyond unilateral initiatives, including Spain on behalf of the European Union, which spoke of the need for the swift start of negotiations "on an effectively verifiable agreement on drastic reductions" of TNWs. The NAC, as well as Finland (on behalf of itself and Sweden) also made strong statements on the issue, and Germany introduced an important working paper on "Non-Strategic Nuclear Weapons". The German paper provides the most detailed analysis and recommendations for reductions in TNWs yet generated in the context of the NPT Review Process. The views of States advocating TNW disarmament also were reflected prominently in the "Chairman's Factual Summary", which was appended to the Final Document. Significantly, none of the nuclear weapons States chose publicly to oppose further reductions of TNWs or to express reservations about the Chair's characterization of the attention given to TNWs in his summary.

Endnotes

* An earlier version of this paper was presented at the UNIDIR Workshop on "Additional Measures to Reduce Tactical Nuclear Weapons", United Nations, New York, 24 September 2001.

1. See, for example, William Potter, "Practical Steps for Addressing the Problem of NSNW" in Jeffrey A. Larsen and Kurt J. Klingenberger (eds.), *Controlling Non-Strategic Nuclear Weapons: Obstacles and Opportunities*, Colorado Springs: Colorado's US Air Force Institute for National Security Studies, 2001, pp. 211-227.

CHAPTER 3

TACTICAL NUCLEAR WEAPONS AND TERRORISM

Pavel Podvig

Although the end of Cold War roughly ten years ago fundamentally changed the face of international security, some of its remnants are still posing arms control difficulties. One such remnant is tactical nuclear weapons (TNWs). TNWs were one of the cornerstones of the confrontation between the United States and the Soviet Union, and one of the first types of weapons to be slated for reduction as the Cold War came to an end. Today, it is important to examine the difficulties of TNW reductions, especially as these may shed light on the problems of verification, transparency and the essential political issues, that will condition the future of arms control between the two former rivals.

To begin the discussion, it is important to recognise that TNWs have no actual military utility. This is especially true if we consider the TNWs currently stationed by the United States in Europe. Neither the European countries nor the United States have made a secret of the fact that the primary reason, perhaps the only one, for having TNWs in Europe is that they help bind NATO together. In basic terms, for the United States and the European countries, TNWs play solely a political role. The pertinent question is whether this role still has any significance.

The situation in Russia is very similar to the one in Europe except that a greater number of Russian analysts believe that TNWs may indeed have a legitimate and useful military role to play. This belief is reminiscent of the old Cold War confrontational style of thinking, which maintains that nuclear weapons can compensate for conventional inferiority. This basic argument continues to be used by the Russian military. It is, however, plainly wrong, and Russia should not continue to rely on nuclear weapons to compensate for the deterioration of its conventional forces. The Russian Federation does not need TNWs any more than does any other country. Whatever the inferiority of Russian conventional forces, there is no reasonable justification for using or even threatening to use TNWs in compensation.

TNWs, however, do play another significant role for Russia, one that is similar to the role they play in the relationship between the United States and NATO. Although perhaps not apparent, Russia sees various aspects of its TNWs policy as an asset and even as a bargaining chip in the various arrangements and negotiations with Europe. The current situation is such that Russia has incentives to retain this political function for its TNWs. For instance, the expansion of NATO is of major concern to Russia. Russia feels increasingly excluded from the new European security arrangements, and although it wants to participate, it believes that it is being kept from doing so. Accordingly, Russia wrongly assumes that TNWs can be used to leverage its way into these security arrangements.

Whatever the role envisaged for nuclear weapons, it is probably strategic. This underscores the fact that there are problems associated with the quantity of TNWs that Russia as well as the United States currently posses. As long as it is not known for example, how many of these weapons Russia has, where they are located, what plans Russia has for them as well as their specific capabilities, the situation will be plagued by uncertainty. At the same time it is important to underscore that Russia is unlikely to agree to a TNWs transparency regime, unless it obtains something valuable in return.

The present situation is clear. The two sides, Russia and the United States, each value TNWs for purely political reasons. Discussions on TNWs can advance only if these particular reasons are addressed. For example, Russia considers the lack of transparency with respect to its TNWs arsenal as one of its most important assets. In other words, Moscow would not favour disclosing the location and number of its TNWs as a means of opening a dialogue with the United States. Nevertheless, Russia may possibly be convinced to agree to certain transparency measures as part of a broader political deal. That said, if the United States and NATO value the presence of American TNWs in Europe so highly that they are unwilling to engage in discussions on this, then the Russian Federation should be excused for valuing its TNWs just as much.

Experience shows that many of the technical problems associated with TNWs can be addressed relatively easily. However, the state of TNWs is driven primarily by political rather than military considerations. This means that whatever solutions to the problem of TNWs are eventually devised, these will by necessity have to be essentially of a political character rather than solely a technical one.

CHAPTER 4

FUEL FOR THE FIRE: TACTICAL NUCLEAR WEAPONS AND TERRORISM

Alistair Millar

After the attacks on the World Trade Center and the Pentagon on 11 September, the United States recruited allies and newly found friends in an effort to formulate options for any retaliatory strikes. United States Secretary of Defense Donald Rumsfeld noted that retaliation would be "unconventional", citing the use of special forces and other less traditional means of dealing with a new type of enemy that is characterised by elusiveness. He also refused to rule out the possibility that an arsenal of tactical nuclear weapons (TNWs) could be used as a component in what was declared as a war against terrorism.[1] Larry Johnson, a former terrorism expert at the State Department, joined a growing chorus of analysts who elaborated on that point in the aftermath of the tragedy by noting that "the options are everything from conventional air strikes to cruise missiles up to and including tactical nuclear weapons".[2]

The term tactical nuclear weapon refers to a broad array of atomic explosive weapons. These range from so-called nuclear landmines and nuclear artillery shells to air-dropped or missile-launched nuclear warheads. Their yields vary from a relative low of 0.1 kiloton to slightly higher than those of the bombs dropped on Hiroshima and Nagasaki. The type of TNWs that have been recommended for optional use as part of the response to the 11 September attacks on the United States would be Earth-penetrating, or "bunker buster" weapons.

Any response by the United States involving the use of TNWs has far-reaching and serious negative consequences and should be rejected for a number of reasons.

First, the use of Earth-penetrating TNWs in the war against terrorism is being suggested because it would allow the United States to reach Osama Bin Laden and, as the case may be, Saddam Hussein who are assumed to be hiding in deeply buried underground bunkers. Some outspoken defence analysts that strongly influence United States policy incorrectly assert that attacking hardened, buried targets with Earth-penetrating nuclear weapons with smaller blast yields, would not harm innocent civilians.

"The use of any nuclear weapon capable of destroying a buried target that is otherwise immune to conventional attack will necessarily produce enormous numbers of civilian casualties", writes Dr. Robert Nelson, a professor of theoretical science at Princeton University, in a recent study for the Federation of American Scientists. "No Earth-burrowing missile can penetrate deep enough in the Earth to contain an explosion with a nuclear yield even as small as 1 percent of the 15-kiloton Hiroshima weapon. The explosion simply blows out a crater of radioactive dirt, which rains down on the local region with an especially intense and deadly fallout".

One can also get a sense of the possible effects of smaller nuclear weapons detonations by looking the United States Department of Defense's own description of what the use of a nuclear weapon by terrorists would entail. It would likely be against "either a military installation or a political target (i.e., the seat of government, large population center, or commercial port city). In such a scenario, citizens outside the immediate lethal area would be exposed to the prompt radiation of the initial explosion as well as to chronic exposures resulting from the residual radioactive fallout".[3]

Second, TNWs pose unique dangers as weapons of terror. Their often-smaller size increases their portability and vulnerability to theft by hostile and potentially hostile groups. Moreover, their unique characteristics of command and control—such as pre-delegated launch authorisation, and often-inadequate safeguards like ineffective permissive action links—add to their potential unauthorised, accidental, or illicit use. A nuclear detonation in New York, Washington, or elsewhere could produce devastation exponentially worse than the incomprehensible destruction we are coping with now. Beyond the tremendous initial damage, rescue efforts in the tragic aftermath would be made utterly impossible because of nuclear contamination.

Third, TNWs contribute to a dangerous notion that they are "useable nukes", lowering the overall nuclear threshold and undermining efforts toward non-proliferation.

Despite these concerns, calls for the development of new types of TNWs in the United States have emerged, largely from analysts at nuclear weapons laboratories. For example, while in his former position at the Los Alamos National Laboratory, United States director of Threat Reduction, Stephen Younger, argued in support of the feasibility and operational usefulness of so-called "mini-nukes". According to Younger, these low-yield nuclear warheads would be deployed on specially configured Earth-penetrating bombs or missiles to target deeply buried or hardened underground targets, such as bunkers and bomb shelters.

Indeed, the United States Congress has even taken some initiative in exploring the development of mini-nukes for deployment in the United States armed services. Republican Senators John Warner of Virginia and Wayne Allard of Colorado have added a provision to the 2001 Defense Authorization Bill that requires the Departments of Energy and Defense to conduct a new study on the use of nuclear weapons for the primary purpose of destroying "hard and deeply buried targets". This study may eventually lead to the overturning of the current congressional ban—the Furse-Spratt provision to the fiscal year 1994 Defense Authorization Bill—prohibiting nuclear laboratories from engaging in research that could lead to the development of a low-yield nuclear weapon.

This prohibition recognises the dangers of plans that signal the intent to develop new TNWs, and acknowledges the possibility of a nuclear backlash against the United States following the use of such weapons. It also recognises the incentive that plans to develop new types of TNWs would give to other countries an incentive to develop nuclear weapons of their own, adding to the problem of increased proliferation. As stated by Rep. Mike Thompson (CA):

> ... developing such a weapon is that it is likely to encourage military and political leaders to think more readily about using nuclear weapons. In my view, we should not lower this threshold or make nuclear weapons a more acceptable choice in war. In addition, development of such a weapon is contrary to our Nation's goals of reducing and eventually eliminating nuclear weapons. To begin development and stockpiling of

> a new nuclear weapon would reverse the difficult achievements the United States has made to slow the proliferation of nuclear material and weapons.[4]

Efforts underway from Senator Warner to overturn Furse-Spratt in order to resume testing and development of "low-yield" nuclear weapons should therefore be viewed as a potentially destabilising.

Would Decision-Makers Actually Ever Use TNWs?

There have been requests in the United Sates Energy Budget by the Bush administration to fund a preliminary study on modifying nuclear warheads for military "bunker busting" operations, but this is not a clear indication that the President would intend to use such a weapon. Such a study may help the administration to assess the negative effects of using this type of weapon, or, conversely it could lead to a program of development and possible testing of new or modified nuclear weapons.

Do these previous circumstances and decisions have much bearing on the future, as the nature of military conflicts has changed? TNWs could have been employed in combat in several instances in the past, but policymakers and military decision-makers decided against their use. Most notably, during the Korean War the United States faced several factors that would have potentially justified the use of TNWs but opted against doing so. In today's context, however, clearer roles have been defined and suggested for the use of a low-yield TNW to penetrate deeply buried bunkers that hitherto have been targets for conventional ballasted penetrator weapons in conflicts in Afghanistan and Iraq. The potential military use for nuclear versions of these penetrating weapons will have to be carefully weighed against important factors before their use would be contemplated. The environmental damage and human casualties will have to be taken into account, as will the international political reaction and the wider consequences upon non-proliferation objectives. In other words, the argument for the political use of TNWs has been weakened in the post-Cold War era by a greater need to stem proliferation by reducing the political value of nuclear weapons.

Since 11 September pundits and former government officials have called for a role for TNWs in the war against terrorism. One answer to these calls and to those by the United States weapons laboratories for a leaner, more usable nuclear weapons arsenal, is that the domestic and international political fallout of a decision to use TNWs would be so extreme as to make the costs of such use much too high. In addition to being a devastating rejection of international norms, American global moral leadership would be thoroughly undermined and would "provide a potent focus for simmering anti-US resentments around the world", undermining United States' national security over the long run.[5]

CONCLUSION

For the past 34 years nuclear non-proliferation policies have established a framework of norms that have helped to prevent a nuclear attack of terror. The United States has been a leader in preventing the spread of nuclear weapons in the past, by pledging to reduce and eventually eliminate its nuclear weapons. It has signed treaties and successfully encouraged other nations to forswear their nuclear programmes. Bending to temptation to threaten to use nuclear weapons will undermine years of work to prevent the spread of nuclear weapons. This is at a time when the vulnerability of the United States to terror attacks has never been clearer.

The multilateral spirit of resolve and cooperation expressed in the international community after 11 September should be seized as a means to expand upon nations' mutual interest in non-proliferation. One of the things that 11 September ought to conjure, should be a profound reminder of the importance of continuing efforts at nuclear arms control. Currently, the United States is joined by the nations of the world in reeling at the horror of what has occurred, and enjoys generous offers of cooperation and commitment to stemming terrorism. This should serve as a startling reminder of the need to continue to work on multilateral, cooperative efforts at arms control. A policy of reliance on and development of new nuclear bombs will only destroy any hope of meaningful cooperation with a world community that shares our concerns and vulnerabilities.

Endnotes

1. On ABC television's "This Week" programme on Sunday 17 September, Secretary of Defense Donald Rumsfeld refused to rule out the use of tactical nuclear weapons.
2. William Neikirk and Steve Hedges, "Talk of Retaliation Includes War; Bin Laden is Suspected as Perpetrator", *Sun-Sentinel*, Fort Lauderdale, FL, 12 September 2001, p. 20A; Another "22 year veteran intelligence officer", expounds: "At a bare minimum, tactical nuclear capabilities should be used against Bin Laden camps in the dessert in Afghanistan" see Thomas Woodrow's op-ed, "Time to Use the Nuclear Option", *The Washington Times*, 14 September 2001 on the internet at http://www.washtimes.com/op-ed/20010914-87723680.htm.
3. United Sates Department of Defense, "Threats, Countermeasures, Technical Barrers, and Accomplishments", in *Chemical and Biological Defense Program: Annual Report to Congress,* March 2000, available online at http://www.defenselink.mil/pubs/chembio02012000.pdf, 11 October 2001.
4. Statement by Rep. Mike Thompson (CA) Congressional Record, 11 October 2000;
http://www.fcnl.org/issues/arm/sup/min_stmthompsn_101100.htm.
5. http://www.lasg.org/wjatsmew/whatsnew2_b.html.

CHAPTER 5

SECURITY OF NUCLEAR MATERIALS AND PAKISTAN'S NUCLEAR WEAPONS

Frank von Hippel

SECURITY OF NUCLEAR-WEAPONS MATERIALS

In the wake of the 11 September events, two of my colleagues and I wrote a letter (attached) to the Presidents of the United States and Russia, and to the Director and Delegates to the General Conference of the International Atomic Energy Agency (IAEA).

The thrust of the letter is that the international community must re-commit itself to securing, consolidating and reducing stockpiles of nuclear-weapon-usable fissile materials and to assuring that redundant weapons experts are able to convert to non-weapons work.

We wrote this letter because we felt that the ongoing efforts in these areas have lost a sense of urgency, become bureaucratic and have often become victims of competing budgetary priorities.

The letter itemizes some of the areas in which we believe that a renewed commitment, increased sense of urgency and greater funding are required.

SECURITY OF PAKISTAN'S NUCLEAR WEAPONS

The Bush-Gorbachev 1991 initiatives grew out of concerns about the fate of nuclear weapons in a disintegrating Soviet Union. At the time,

Secretary of State James Baker said that the United States concern was that the Soviet Union could turn into "a Yugoslavia with nukes".

Today, some of us are worried about the possibility that Pakistan, under the pressure of being used as a base for a United States campaign against terrorists in Afghanistan, could be taken over by fundamentalists as Iran was—potentially turning it into an "Afghanistan with nukes".

Pakistan's nuclear weapons are likely to share the vulnerabilities of some Soviet and American TNWs in 1991: accessibility, portability and lack of coded use controls.

On 16 September, Vice President Cheney was asked about the concerns of the United States government over the security of Pakistan's nuclear weapons. He responded that: "You could have a change of government in relatively short notice, and we're well aware of that".[1]

Last year Pakistan reportedly requested foreign help, including from the United States, to improve what it calls the "custodial safeguards" of its nuclear weapons. The Clinton administration declined to help Pakistan, so as not to legitimize its nuclear capability. The Bush administration is reconsidering this position but has stressed that delivering assistance would take some time—if it is possible to get an agreement with Pakistan on specifics at all.[2]

In any case, if there were a real coup, including the change of allegiance of the personnel or guards at Pakistan's nuclear facilities, improved security against external attack or unauthorized actions might not help.

According to one non-governmental expert, George Perkovich, Pakistan has two to three dozen potential nuclear warheads, all based on highly-enriched uranium. He believes that, in normal times, Pakistan keeps the warheads separate from the missiles and aircraft that would be used to deliver them. Furthermore, he believes that the fissile uranium core of the weapon is kept separate from the electronics and high-explosives that make up the remainder of the warhead. He believes that each part is well guarded, in secure storage.[3]

Under these circumstances, of greatest concern would be the fissile cores—especially because they are made of weapon-grade uranium (WgU). WgU, unlike plutonium, can be used in a gun-type nuclear weapon design—something that is well within the capability of a sub-national group. In a gun-type design, one subcritical piece of WgU is fired down a gun-barrel into another subcritical piece to create a supercritical mass in which a neutron chain reaction is then initiated.

The Hiroshima bomb was a gun-type weapon. It was so simple that it was not tested. However, a gun-type design requires more WgU than an implosion device, in which a subcritical core of fissile material is imploded to a smaller, denser, supercritical mass. According to David Albright's description of the South African gun-type designs, each device weighed about a ton, had a diameter of 0.65 m, a length of 1.8 m and contained about 55 kg of WgU. The estimated yield was 10-18 kilotons.[4] So, if the cores of Pakistan's weapons contained 20 kg of WgU each, then, it would take 3 complete cores to make a gun-type weapon.

Pakistan apparently fears that India or Israel—or perhaps the United States—might try to eliminate its nuclear weapons during this crisis. This concern was apparent in General Musharraf's speech of 19 September:[5]

> Pakistan's army and every Pakistani will defend Pakistan with everything she's got—her strategic assets... At this point, the whole air force is on high alert, and everybody's on a do-or-die mission.

The code word, "strategic assets", refers to Pakistan's nuclear weapons and the aircraft and missiles that could deliver them. They are seen as vital to Pakistan's survival.

A key question is whether, in preparing the Air Force for a "do-or-die mission", the nuclear warheads have been assembled as a deterrent against possible attack.

It seems exceedingly unlikely that, in case of attack by fundamentalists, Pakistan's government would be willing to turn its nuclear weapons over to another government before it is too late to do so.[6]

Under the circumstances, what can be done?

Arguably, if American-Pakistani consultations on this question are not already under way, they should be undertaken. These discussions should make at least following points clear:

1. As long as the government of Pakistan maintains clear control over its nuclear weapons—i.e., they are not in danger of falling under the control of fundamentalists—they will not be attacked.
2. Pakistan must keep its warheads dismantled and their components in secure bunkers.
3. Pakistan should stop producing highly-enriched uranium and separated plutonium.
4. Individuals with potential fundamentalist sympathies must be screened out of groups in contact with or guarding nuclear-weapons components or fissile materials.
5. Finally, Pakistan should assure that its weapons and highly-enriched uranium would be destroyed before they could fall into the hands of fundamentalists.

In particular, preparations should be made to rapidly mix the weapon-grade uranium with natural or depleted uranium to reduce its enrichment to well below the 20 percent threshold of weapon-usability.[7]

Endotes

1. Bryan Bender, "US Considers Helping Pakistan", *Boston Globe*, 20 September 2001, http://www.boston.com/dailyglobe2/263/nation/US_considers_helping_PakistanP.shtml.
2. Ibid.
3. Nigel Hawkes, "The Nuclear Threat: Pakistan Could Lose Control of its Arsenal", *The Times*, 20 September 2001, http://www.thetimes.co.uk/article/0,,2001320010-2001324777,00.html.
4. David Albright, "South African and the Affordable Bomb", *Bulletin of the Atomic Scientists*, July/August 1994, p. 37.
5. Remarks by Pakistani President Pervez Musharraf to the Pakistani People, " The United States and the Response to Last Week's Terrorist Attacks", Federal News Service, Islamabad, Pakistan, 19 September 2001, http://web.lexis-nexis.com/universe/document?_m=bf5af4d86fc346ba682529644ae447df&_docnum=19&wchp=

dGLStV-ISIAl&_md5=458ec3764f66daa5468588a4fdd07a45.

6. One suggestion is that China might volunteer to hold Pakistan's fissile material for safekeeping.
7. One way might be to chip and then oxidize the metal WgU components in small oil-heated air-blown furnace with filters and then mix it with natural or depleted uranium oxide. One of the seminar participants, Richard Garwin, suggested as a quicker alternative that the WgU metal and separate natural or depleted uranium metal could be quickly melted and allowed to flow together in a mixing vessel. He suggested that a ready source of energy for this process could be the "thermite" reaction, in which a mixture of ferric iron oxide and aluminum powder would be poured around the uranium metal, the setup buried in sand and ignited in the reaction: Fe_2O_3 + 2Al ö2Fe + Al_2O_3 (214 grams/mole). The energy release in the reaction is roughly 3,750 joules/gram and produces molten iron at a temperature above 2,500°C (the melting point of iron is 1,540°C). The melting temperature of uranium is 1,135°C and the heat required to bring it from ambient temperature to melting is about 130 joules/gram. The heat loss required to cool a mixture of molten iron and aluminum oxide from 2,500°C down to the melting point of uranium is about 800 joules per gram. Even allowing for heat losses, it would therefore probably require less than one gram of thermite mixture to melt one gram of uranium. The design of any such a rapid uranium de-enrichment process would have to be developed and tested experimentally with low-enriched uranium before implementation. For obvious reasons, more than one critical mass should not be melted together.

   It might be easier to persuade Pakistan to carry this out if the dilution was to 20 percent. Then 82 percent of the WgU could be recovered at a cost of only 5 percent of the separating work originally required to produce it. [Enriching 20 percent U back up to 90 percent with 5 percent tails and Feed/Product = 5.667 would recover 82 percent of the original WgU at a cost of 5 percent of the separation work units originally invested to produce the WgU (9.4 SWU/kg vs 195 SWU/kg for enriching from 0.7 percent with 0.3 percent tails and Feed/Product = 224.25.]

ANNEX

Letter of 19 September 2001 with regard to the urgency of expanded commitments to cooperative nuclear weapons and materials security and conversion programs

George W. Bush, President of the United States
The White House
1600 Pennsylvania Avenue, NW
Washington, DC 20500
USA

Vladimir V. Putin, President of the Russian Federation
The Kremlin
Moscow, 103073
Russian Federation

Director General Mohamed El-Baradei and IAEA General Conference Delegates
International Atomic Energy Agency
P.O. Box 100
Wagramer Strasse 5
A-1400 Vienna, Austria

Dear President Bush, President Putin, Dr. El-Baradei, and Delegates to the General Conference of the International Atomic Energy Agency,

We are appalled by the terrorist attacks last week in New York and Washington DC. Our sympathies are with the innocent victims and their families and friends. But we are also extremely alarmed by this event. There can now be little doubt that if such terrorists obtain weapons of mass destruction in the future they will use them. It is imperative, therefore, that preventing terrorists from gaining access to the technologies and materials of weapons of mass destruction—including nuclear materials—be a high priority component of the new global battle against terrorism.

Such an effort must ensure that all weapons-usable nuclear materials worldwide are secure and accounted for, to stringent standards. The United States and Russia, as the holders of the largest stockpiles, bear a special responsibility to re-double their cooperation to secure and control nuclear warheads, materials, technology and expertise. But in a world with knowledgeable and well-organized terrorist groups with global reach, inadequately secured nuclear material anywhere is a threat to all nations everywhere. Therefore, we call on all countries to increase their attention and financial and political support to these vital efforts as well.

Unfortunately, over the past five years, many of the major United States-Russian cooperative nuclear security programs have slowed, and many activities have been under-funded or had their timelines unnecessarily extended into the future. Bureaucratic disputes, disagreements on levels of access to facilities, and other political differences have eroded the vital United States-Russian nonproliferation partnership, hampering the implementation of many important international security programs.

But recent events have underscored the urgency of this mission and the demand for accelerated action. This will require increasing the pace and the scale of efforts to ensure that all warheads and potential bomb material are secure and accounted for, and that excess scientists and engineers with expertise relating to nuclear-weapons production receive effective conversion assistance.

We call on Russia, the United States, and the other nations attending the International Atomic Energy Agency (IAEA) General Conference this week in Vienna, to commit the resources necessary to achieve these goals in the shortest possible period of time.

The United States, Russia, and the rest of the international community should move urgently to take the following steps:

- Expand cooperative material protection, control and accounting (MPC&A) activities in Russia. The United States-Russian program is now entering its eighth year. However, by the end of 2001, security upgrades will have been completed on less than 40 percent of the over 600 metric tons of highly-enriched uranium (HEU) and plutonium in the former Soviet Union located outside Russia's nuclear weapons stockpiles. And completion of the upgrades is not expected before 2010. Expanded funding is necessary to speed the overall pace of the effort, consolidate the nuclear materials into fewer facilities, initiate performance testing of installed security systems under a variety of threat scenarios, and to ensure that the security systems are maintained and sustained. The goal should be to ensure that all weapons-usable nuclear material is sustainably secured and accounted for as rapidly as technologically possible.

- Expand international cooperative efforts to interdict illicit trafficking of nuclear and other weapons of mass destruction materials and technologies, including increasing intelligence assets focused on this threat and expanding the sharing of intelligence.

- Expand international cooperative efforts to ensure high levels of security and accounting for nuclear material around the world—in particular doubling or tripling the budget of the IAEA's International Physical Protection Advisory Service.

- Move forward rapidly to place all plutonium and HEU no longer required for military purposes under IAEA verification, including reaching agreement rapidly on the specific arrangements and necessary resources.

- Accelerate efforts to reduce stockpiles of potentially vulnerable nuclear material, including accelerating the blend-down of excess highly-enriched uranium, and expediting the disposition of excess weapons plutonium. The United States and Russia have declared their joint intention to dispose of 68 metric tons of this plutonium but the disposition program has stalled over cost concerns and other issues. We urge the international community to provide the resources and leadership necessary to move quickly to reduce global stockpiles of excess plutonium.

- Undertake data exchanges among IAEA members on national nuclear material stockpiles, which would be updated regularly.

- Greatly increase help to Russia in downsizing its nuclear weapons complex and converting excess weapons workers to civilian work or helping them retire. While the United States has significantly reduced its nuclear weapons complex, Russia still maintains an enormous and unstable complex that has changed little since the end of the Cold War. Russia has stated that it wants to downsize this complex, but greater and more effective international support is necessary for alternative employment for the thousands of workers that will be displaced.

It is our sincere hope that the recent tragedy will galvanize accelerated and effective international action in these areas in the coming months and years. The inadequate funding and bureaucratic, administrative, and political disagreements that have slowed nuclear security cooperation in recent years seem petty in comparison to the devastating loss of life last week. We call on Russia, the United States, and the international community to renew their efforts to keep weapons of mass destruction from falling into the wrong hands.

Sincerely,

Matthew Bunn
Assistant Director
Science, Technology, and Public Policy Program
Harvard University
Former Advisor to White House Office of Science and Technology Policy

Kenneth N. Luongo
Executive Director
Russian American Nuclear Security Advisory Council (RANSAC)
Former Director, Office of Arms Control and Nonproliferation, US Department of Energy

Frank N. von Hippel
Professor of Public and International Affairs
Princeton University
Former Assistant Director for National Security, White House Office of Science and Technology Policy

PART II

Strengthening the 1991 Declarations

CHAPTER 6

TACTICAL NUCLEAR ARMS CONTROL?[1]

Alexander A. Pikayev

The rapid decline of Russia's conventional military might since the disintegration of the Soviet Union in 1991 has understandably led to a growing emphasis on the country's still powerful nuclear arsenal for protecting it and its allies from nuclear and large scale conventional attack. In the course of the 1990s this new emphasis together with deteriorating Russian-Western political relations prevented radical steps towards nuclear disarmament. The sizeable and unprecedented nuclear reductions witnessed during the last decade took place thanks to unilateral and bilateral decisions made in early the 1990s[2] and Russia's economic hardships. Since the Strategic Arms Reduction Treaties (START) I and II were signed in 1991 and 1993 respectively, no new major disarmament accord between Russia and the United Sates has been reached.

In the area of tactical nuclear weapons (TNWs) no formal arms control regime was negotiated, although Russia and the United States continued to abide by the unilateral declarations made by presidents Bush and Gorbachev in the fall of 1991 whose implementation had been nearly completed by the year 2000. Due to these unilateral initiatives, the field deployments of TNWs has decreased dramatically with thousands of warheads being destroyed annually by each side. Russia withdrew all TNWs to its national territory, while the United States has significantly reduced its TNWs deployments in Europe.

Nevertheless, the unilateral declarations have never been codified into legally binding arms control provisions. As a result, they remain non-verifiable and reversible. There is also no confidence in whether they have been fully implemented by the end of 2000, as originally mandated. The 2001 controversy around the possible transfer of Russian TNWs to

Kaliningrad has shown that codifying the unilateral declarations still meets security interests of, at least, European nations.

The lack of momentum on further nuclear disarmament has became a subject of international concern; this was reflected in particular during the 2000 Non-Proliferation Treaty (NPT) Review Conference. Together with a long stalemate in the United States-Russian START/Anti-Ballistic Missiles (ABM) process and its partial collapse in 2001, the lack of a formal TNWs control regime has increased mutual suspicions about the potential reversibility of the existing unilateral pledges and self-restrains. At the same time, the possibility of establishing a formal TNWs control regime—which could be the biggest achievement in United States-Russian nuclear arms control in coming decade—faces a complicated combination of opportunities and challenges and thus remains uncertain. Fortunately, certain recent developments have provided some hopes that the establishment of a formal TNWs control regime remains within the realm of the possible.

2000 THREAT REASSESSMENT AND ROLE OF NUCLEAR WEAPONS

Soon after coming to power in 2000, President Vladimir Putin's new administration began an in-depth process of re-evaluation of Russia's foreign and security priorities. This review concluded that the real and present danger for Russian security comes from low intensity conflicts emerging along Russia's vulnerable underbelly stretching from the Black Sea to the Pamir Mountains. Although relations with other powerful neighbours in the East and West are not free of controversy, the security challenges emanating from there are not as acute and immediate.

Unlike the Soviet Union, Russia possesses very limited resources. While in Soviet times Moscow could spend, under some estimates, up to $100 billion, in 2002 the overall size of the Russian federal budget is expected at no more than $50 billion. Though in 2002 national defence spending will increase to a level of approximately 280 billion rubles, it will still remain at a level of mere $9.2 billion (using the average expected 2002 exchange rate) or about 2.5 percent of the United States FY02 defence budget.

With such resources the Kremlin simply cannot afford to continue an all azimuths policy of confrontation, such as it conducted twenty years ago. Instead, the Putin administration wants to concentrate on recent threats—the conflicts in the Caucasus and Central Asia. At the same time, it expects to solve less tense and more hypothetical problems with Eastern and especially Western neighbours, by diplomatic means with minimal defence allocations.

In 2000, to the surprise of outside observers, Moscow began to consider de-emphasising the importance of nuclear weapons in its general security policy. A part of the military establishment fingers the disproportional high percentage of Russia's defence procurement budget spent on the nuclear forces. According to the data provided by official military sources, in 1999 the nuclear share reached 90 percent of the entire Defence Ministry procurement. Reportedly, in 2000 the attempt to reach a more balanced distribution of spending on nuclear and conventional forces (50 percent on each), failed. Minuscule conventional procurement prevents the military from buying arms and equipment urgently needed for the Chechen war and for dealing with the deteriorating security situation in Central Asia.

Based on public information, the plan for military reform drafted by the General Staff of the Russian Armed Forces in summer 2000, requires a gradual improvement of conventional forces at the expense of nuclear ones. By 2016, conventional forces are expected to be capable of providing credible non-nuclear deterrence. In the short term, they are to be capable of fighting two regional wars. The expenditures needed to reach these goals are to come from savings achieved through the further reduction of manpower and of nuclear deployments in particular. According to the plan, Moscow is to reduce dramatically its strategic nuclear weapons within next few years, and downsize its nuclear modernisation programs. The Strategic Rocket Forces (SRF), which still controls the bulk of Russia's strategic weapons, might be abolished as a separate armed service. The strength of the SRF is to be reduced significantly. Reportedly, levels of deployed TNWs are be maintained at a few thousand warheads.

The relative de-emphasis of nuclear weapons came through during the debates on Russia's new military doctrine. In a draft military doctrine published in November 1993, Moscow officially disavowed the long-standing Soviet declaratory policy on the no-first-use of nuclear weapons, although the use of nuclear weapons continued to be envisaged as a matter of last resort. In 1999, after the war in Kosovo, Russian military leaders made several statements which might be regarded as their commitment to early nuclear first use—that is, use during the initial phases of a conflict or even in case of crisis. That produced widespread expectations that the new military doctrine drafted by 2000 might reflect a more nuclearised Russian military thinking.

In fact, the debates in early 2000 on the new doctrine showed that the nuclearising trends registered in 1999 have been reversed. The war in Chechnya, which began in August 1999, demonstrated the futility of nuclear might against threats such as separatism, radicalism and international terrorism. The National Security concept, signed by President Putin on 6 January 2000, did not clarify further the role of nuclear weapons in Russia's security policy. Furthermore, the military doctrine, which after painful debates was finally adopted in May 2000, reinstated the basic nuclear provisions of the 1993 doctrine, that nuclear weapons could be used only after all other tools to halt hostilities have failed. Thus, the 1999 concerns about Russia's transition towards an early first-use option have not materialised.

It is not clear whether the decisions made in 2000 will eventually be implemented in their reported form. Developments in 2001 demonstrated, that opposition inside the Russian military establishment to a denuclearised defence posture has considerably weakened. The resignation of Marshal Sergeyev from the position of Defence Minister was accompanied by the demotion of the SRF from one of three major armed services and to the role of separate forces (*rod voysk*) subordinated to the General Staff. In late 2000, the Kremlin also made clear its desire to proceed with radical strategic arms reductions to a level of 1,000 deployed warheads.

Whether the recent denuclearisation in Russian military thinking represents a long-term trend remains an open question. Difficulties in improving the conventional deterrent in the short term might prevent the de-emphasis of nuclear forces in practice. Moreover, the low strength of the ground forces whose manpower is expected to fall to 170,000 troops, means that in the future, the conventional forces might not be able to counteract conventional intrusions by mid-size powers, like Iran or Turkey. Therefore, the reduced nuclear arsenals will likely be even more important as a weapon of last resort in defending national territory—or what was national territory less than ten years ago. Nuclear weapons thus will not only maintain their relevance in Russia's military relations with the North Atlantic Treaty Organisation (NATO) and China, but their perceived significance will proliferate to regional levels.

Hypothetically, if recent trends continue, growing conventional regional imbalances in the South could provoke a shift in priorities inside the nuclear forces. At the moment, strategic missions play more important roles. However, a need to provide deterrence against regional adversaries might lead to an increasing importance of TNWs. Targeting list of strategic ballistic missiles could be also modified in order to include certain Asian targets. Finally, heavy nuclear-armed bombers might be also used to conduct regional operations.

Although in 2000-2001 the Russian leadership sincerely wanted to lessen the nuclear emphasis of the last decade, the continuing presence of severe budgetary restrictions for conventional military procurement together with the inability to establish better political relations with the West might force it to return to a nuclear emphasis in its general defence posture. If that happens, non-strategic nuclear missions could become more important than they were in the 1990s. Consequently, role of TNWs would increase further.

At the same time, should the involvement of the United States and other Western nations in Central Asia and the South Caucasus help to establish a more favourable security environment in the South and a broader Russian-Western cooperative security system, the need for a greater regional role for nuclear weapons might abate. The strategic deterrent would also play a decreasing role in relations with the West. This could allow a considerable breakthrough in non-strategic nuclear disarmament, including the possible conclusion of formal disarmament pledges.

INTERDEPENDENCE BETWEEN TACTICAL AND STRATEGIC NUCLEAR ARMS CONTROL

Beyond certain recent political opportunities, the prospects for establishing a formal TNWs control regime depend on the future of United

States-Russian bilateral strategic arms control. In December 2001 the United States formally notified the Russian Federation of its intent to withdrawal from the ABM Treaty in June 2002. The decision caused widespread international regret. At the same time, Russia and the United States have agreed to resume their bilateral strategic arms reductions dialogue, which was interrupted in 2000 prior to the United States presidential elections. There are real prospects that the two sides could conclude a new legally binding agreement on deep strategic nuclear reductions before the ABM Treaty is formally abrogated in June 2002. Therefore, the United States-Russian bilateral strategic arms control process might be partially repaired and the negative consequences of the withdrawal from the ABM Treaty might be partially neutralised.

Moreover, the 2002 agreement on deep strategic nuclear reductions might open the door to establishing the new strategic framework for relations between Moscow and Washington so desperately needed after the end of the Cold War. Particularly, the two sides could find solutions to several complicated issues such questions of transparency and verification of future deep nuclear reductions, and more importantly, their irreversibility.

Russia's concerns over reversibility are linked to the fact that the United States is going to reduce its nuclear stockpiles primarily through downloading and storage rather than the physical elimination of warheads. These could then be reinstalled on delivery vehicles relatively quickly (i.e., a matter of weeks). Most likely, except for 50 *MX Peacekeeper* Intercontinental Ballistic Missiles (ICBMs), United States is not going to decommission any other strategic nuclear delivery vehicles. Reductions carried out in such a manner can hardly be considered as real disarmament. They might rather be called partial de-alerting of strategic nuclear arsenals. The number of decommissioned nuclear warheads which could be returned to operational status might be as high as 4,000. Together with the forces slated to remain operational (1,700-2,200 strategic warheads), the overall numbers of strategic warheads would remain at the 6,000 ceiling established by the 1991 START I. Russia would face significant problems in maintaining operational levels comparable to those of the United States. For Moscow, it would be very difficult to retain the reserve capabilities the Pentagon wants to keep in ten years.

Theoretically, the reversibility problem could be solved either through the dismantlement of decommissioned strategic nuclear delivery vehicles (SNDVs), or warheads. The United States plans to maintain the carriers operational, or convert them for non-strategic nuclear or non-nuclear missions. Four Ohio-class strategic nuclear submarines will carry sea-launched cruise missiles instead of the *Trident II* Submarine-launched ballistic missiles (SLBMs) they currently deploy. Part of the United States strategic bombers will be converted to carry non-nuclear payloads. The decommissioned MX *Peacekeeper* ICBMs will be, most likely, kept in reserve. Washington will be, most likely, reluctant to destroy converted SNDVs. But even if all converted SNDVs were eliminated, this would not solve the reversibility problem. As a result of downloading, the operational carriers will deploy significantly fewer warheads than they do currently. In ten years, perhaps, up to 2,500 warheads could be uploaded on operational *Trident II* and *Minutemen III* ballistic missiles.

Therefore, the irreversibility of strategic nuclear reductions cannot be achieved through the elimination of decommissioned delivery vehicles alone. Rather, it should be combined with the elimination of decommissioned nuclear warheads. Russia and the United States have already discussed the cooperative, transparent dismantlement of warheads. In the mid-1990s, Washington delivered to Moscow its first proposal of that kind. In the 1997 Helsinki Statement signed during the United States-Russian summit, the two sides agreed to discuss warhead transparency as a potential measure aiming at achieving the irreversibility of strategic nuclear reductions. In January 2000 the United States delivered a proposal regarding warhead transparency during the United States-Russian START III consultations. Russia, however, rejected the proposal.

Partially, Russia's reluctance to deal with warhead transparency was linked to objective technical difficulties in monitoring its stockpiles and warhead elimination. Indeed, all bilateral strategic arms reduction agreements have dealt with delivery vehicles—none have required warhead elimination or transparency. Consequently, the technical monitoring and verification of warheads is not adequately developed, and their bilateral cooperative elaboration could be time consuming.

However, the major concern was probably related to TNWs. Besides dismantlement facilities, verification of irreversible elimination of decommissioned strategic nuclear warheads requires the establishment of verification measures for warhead storage sites. Otherwise irreversibility cannot be ensured. The same sites might contain both strategic and tactical warheads. Therefore, the warhead verification regime aimed at guaranteeing the irreversibility of strategic reductions would inevitable affect tactical nuclear stockpiles, which are not subject to limitations imposed by strategic arms reduction agreements.

It should be mentioned that between 1997-99 the Russians were ready to accept formal TNWs control. In the 1997 Helsinki Statement both the United States and Russia expressed their willingness to discuss tactical nuclear arms and sea-launched cruise missiles in talks to be held parallel to the START III negotiations. In fact, the Helsinki Statement was a package deal. In response to the willingness of the United States to accept good terms for START III, Moscow had to commit itself to TNWs control, something it was unwilling to do before.

Since early 1999, however, the Helsinki package has effectively ceased to exist. In January 1999, the Clinton administration formally proposed to modify the ABM Treaty so as be able to engage in broader testing and potentially deploy a limited national missile defence system (NMD). Also, the administration established a link between Moscow's willingness to modify the ABM Treaty and progress in the START III talks. That meant that TNWs were dropped from the package. Since 1999 the Russians have found the modification of the ABM Treaty too high a price to pay for START III, and they were certainly not going to add to it the control of TNWs. Under the circumstances, Russia was probably concerned that the United States was attempting to sneak TNWs back onto the negotiation agenda through the back door when the latter made its warhead transparency proposal in 2000. The Russians thus rejected the proposal.

The United States decision to withdraw from the ABM Treaty made in December 2001, ironically, re-established the Helsinki linkage between strategic and tactical nuclear arms control in the United States-Russian bilateral diplomatic context. Without the need by United States to gain Moscow's consent on the ABM Treaty, Russia can expect to obtain its goals in strategic arms reduction only by placing its perceived mighty tactical nuclear capabilities on the negotiating table. In practical terms, this was already reflected in early 2002, when the Russians began to talk about the need for warhead elimination in order to ensure the irreversibility of deep strategic nuclear reductions. They had to accept the logic of the Clinton administration, which two years ago seemed so inappropriate.

This significant change of Russia's position on the warhead transparency might open a realistic road towards establishing a formal TNWs control regime. Since Russia and the United States would have to place, at least, part of their tactical nuclear stockpiles under the strategic warhead transparency regime anyway, they would face less constraints in agreeing on other formal and far-reaching TNWs control measures.

The road to TNWs control through strategic warhead transparency would not be easy. Although Russia's current declaratory position favours the idea, there are some grounds to believe that its negotiation position still insists on elimination of delivery vehicles, not warheads as such. The United States, however, with its new administration, has lost most of its interest in both warhead transparency and TNWs control. Technical difficulties in elaborating reliable but not too intrusive verification measures also continue to persist. However, it seems that the only realistic way to achieve formal TNWs control is through continuing the United States-Russian strategic arms reduction talks and particularly, their expansion into the areas of warhead elimination and transparency.

CONCLUSION

In the early 2000s Russian military though took a surprising step away from a nuclearised national defence posture. Several important decisions were made, which have the potential to denuclearise Russia's defence priorities. So far, it remains unclear whether the current trend of denuclearisation will be sustained in the long-term. To a large extent, it depends on the development of relations between Russia and the West. Particularly, if the West helps Russia address its pressing security challenges coming from the South, the rapprochement might influence not only Russia's central strategic nuclear posture, but also Russia's propensity to transport nuclear priorities to the regional level. If this happens, the re-emergence of TNWs in Russian military thought could be halted and substituted with a cooperative security relationship with the West. That would remove a major obstacle to making Russia's TNWs stockpiles more transparent and controllable.

Currently, the pursuit of the United States-Russian strategic arms dialogue represents, maybe, the only practical track for achieving formal TNWs control. The United States should approach Russia's and international concerns on the irreversibility of deep strategic nuclear reductions more creatively. Among other things, the bilateral dialogue on irreversibility would unavoidably lead to discussions of warhead elimination and transparency measures. Today's significant change in Russia's declaratory position regarding verified warhead elimination provides a unique opportunity to expand formal arms control provisions to tactical nuclear warheads. Later, more significant TNWs control measures could be negotiated.

Endotes

1. This paper represents an updated version of the author's presentation at the UNIDIR tactical arms control workshop held in the United Nations in September 2001. It is partially based on author's Memo published by the Program for New Approaches to Russia's Security (recently with the CSIS).
2. Also known as Presidential Nuclear Initiatives.

CHAPTER 7

A REALISTIC STRATEGY FOR CONTROLLING TACTICAL NUCLEAR WEAPONS

Jack Spencer

More than ten years after the end of the Cold War, tactical nuclear weapons (TNWs) retain their two essential roles: deterrence and warfighting. Only the context has changed. The 1991 Gulf War illustrated the important deterrent role of tactical nuclear weapons. Many observers estimate that the threat of nuclear retaliation dissuaded Saddam Hussein from using chemical and biological weapons against either the Allied troops or Israel. Following the terrorist attacks of 11 September against the United States, there is talk about the possible role of TNWs in Afghanistan or elsewhere in the war against States that harbour terrorists. Under current circumstances, TNWs are being considered mainly as a military option. While I do not believe that TNWs will in fact be used, the United States administration is not going to forego this option, and nor ought it. The bottom line is that the deterrent value of a weapon is directly related to the credibility of the threat that it will be used.

Since the 1991 unilateral declarations by former Presidents Bush and Gorbachev, both the United States and Russia have eliminated a large number of TNWs. Nevertheless, the 1991 TNWs regime is still commonly portrayed as weak and inadequate, and there are calls for new and drastic measures to further reduce or perhaps completely eliminate the two countries' TNW arsenals, or for a new multilateral TNWs reduction treaty involving all nuclear-weapon States. I believe that there are substantial difficulties with all of these suggestions and that even if we proceed with the further reduction of TNWs, piling up treaty upon treaty is certainly not an appropriate path to follow.

Let us begin by defining TNWs. It is important to understand that a weapon is tactical by the nature of its use, not by the nature of its design. Arguably, only the United States and Russia truly possess TNWs. These are the only countries that still maintain lower yield nuclear weapons to supplement their conventional combat capabilities. While other nuclear-armed States have or will have lower yield, shorter-range nuclear weapons, these weapons are actually strategic, not tactical and therefore ought not to be subject to the same arms control regime.

As the reduction of TNWs moves forward, the process ought to take two separate forms: a bilateral one between the United States and Russia and, should we wish to address the lower yield, shorter-range nuclear weapons of the other countries, a separate multilateral one. Keeping these two processes distinct will be key to their success. The latter is premised on the understanding that the United States-Russian nuclear relationship is unique, and that adding India and Pakistan or even China, France and Great Britain into the same regime as United States and Russia would be a mistake.

Focusing only the United States-Russian relationship, the idea of reciprocal, unilateral reductions such as those undertaken by Presidents Bush and Gorbachev in 1991, has in fact great merit. A similar approach would actually be better suited for building down strategic arsenals as well. As already noted, however, a number of observers find the current TNWs regime excessively weak and call for strengthening it by concluding a legally binding treaty. While unilateral approaches to arms reductions have their own problems, it is unlikely that becoming entangled in more treaties is a viable solution.

LEARNING FROM THE PAST

Turning to history, there are a few important points we can learn from past arms control treaties. Three of these points can be summarised as follows:

1. *Treaties as Ends, Not Means.* Take for example, the 1972 Anti-Ballistic Missile (ABM) Treaty. This treaty was signed 30 years ago with a State that no longer exists, to manage an international system that has disappeared, to protect the United States against a threat that is

defunct. Yet, the ABM Treaty impedes the United States from defending against a threat that does exist with technology that does exist (but did not at the time). So, why do many analysts still subscribe to the ABM Treaty? The short answer is that the treaty, which perpetuates Cold War thinking, has become an end in itself—it has become its own objective.

2. *Simply Unenforceable*. Enforcement is a general problem plaguing arms control treaties. As long as all parties involved are satiated (but in that case, do we actually need arms control treaties at all?) then everything is all right. However, a nation intent on war will never allow a treaty to stand in its way. Take for example the case of Japan in the inter-war period. Once Japan firmly decided on its policy of rearmament, it simply cast aside its earlier commitments under the Washington Naval Treaty, which it abandoned in 1934. In fact this is how most of the pre-WWII disarmament treaties fell apart.

3. *Unverifiable*. Arms control treaties are notoriously difficult to verify. The problem, most basically, is that those nations that pose the greatest threats are the ones that are least likely to comply with the treaty. For instance, the current discussions over the Protocol on Verification to the Biological and Toxin Weapons Convention (BTWC), are largely a reflection of scepticism over the extent to which the provision of the BTWC are actually verifiable. Moreover, attempts at applying verification simply give rise to a new problem without solving the old one. The new problem is that verification subjects law-abiding democracies to the same scrutiny as vicious dictatorships with no guarantee that the latter will reveal anything. As such, verification does little to promote outcomes that truly will decrease the threat. The best way to do that is to undermine the demand for weapons in the first place.

Arms control treaties, therefore, can fall prey to several flaws in which case they do not work particularly well. So where do we go from here?

WHERE TO GO FROM HERE

It is important to understand that friendly nations should not need arms control treaties. The existence of a treaty presupposes an adversarial relationship at some level. As such, it is imperative not to continue heaping treaty upon treaty upon the United States and Russia in the tradition of the Cold War. Policy has to move beyond the Cold War; the latter is over and Russia is not the enemy. The worst path forward is to engage in a Strategic Arms Reductions Treaty (START)-like process and impose this or that ceiling on the number of TNWs or their delivery systems. Yes, both nations have huge arsenals of ageing TNWs. Neither, however, either needs or wants them! So why are we stuck with them? The most likely answer is that we are stuck in the quagmire of Cold War arms control that perpetuates old thinking.

It is this mentality that has prevented the reciprocal unilateral approach from working as well as it might have. The problem is that analysts remain wed to Cold War notions of arms control, which by its very nature breeds suspicion. If we go down this path, neither the United States nor Russia will ever, in confidence, build down to a minimal number of weapons. We should not rely on these antiquated and obsolete notions of arms control. A structured approach to reduction is certainly needed, but not one that places limits on volume or other aspects. Instead, the structure should revolve around nurturing a relationship between the United States and Russia based on mutual interests such as free trade, the promotion of human rights and the reduction of the number of States producing weapons of mass destruction. Nuclear weapons must no longer be at the centre of this relationship. National interest and good relations will ensure a stable equilibrium. This approach—not a treaty—should result in transparency and monitoring agreements and other confidence-building measures. The latter will help alleviate some of the suspicion and hopefully allow both countries to build down because each will be confident that the other is doing likewise.

CONCLUSION

The best way to reduce the quantity of existing TNWs is to move beyond Cold War-style arms control and through modernisation. As described above, continuing to rely on antiquated notions of arms control impedes reductions by perpetuating the same old thinking that led to the build-ups in the first place. Modernising the current TNWs forces would result in more reliable, more modern and thus smaller arsenals. The existing multitude of TNWs ought to be replaced with a few highly reliable and adaptable weapons. Modernisation ought to be accompanied by a dialogue between the United States and Russia, which would not place limits on TNWs, but rather would create a regime for monitoring and increasing transparency that would facilitate further reciprocal unilateral reductions of both side's ageing stockpiles.

CHAPTER 8

THE CHALLENGED REGIME ON TACTICAL NUCLEAR WEAPONS: DEBATE ON LEGAL ASPECTS

Taina Susiluoto[1]

The worst terrorist attacks in the history of the United States took place on 11 September 2001. Suicide hijackers turned Boeing 757 and 767 airplanes into guided missiles that struck two economic and military symbols of the United States, the World Trade Center towers in New York and the Pentagon building in Washington. This tragic event brought to an end the illusion of American invulnerability.

The events of 11 September united the world in an unprecedented way. Within hours the United Nations Security Council condemned the attacks. For the first time in the history of the North Atlantic Treaty Organisation (NATO), Article 5, which stipulates that an armed attack against one member is considered as an attack against all members, was invoked.[2] Statements presented at the Conference on Disarmament (CD) in Geneva on Thursday, 14 September underscored the fact that these attacks were not directed only against the United States. The Secretary-General of the United Nations Kofi Annan contributed an article to the *New York Times* in which he stated that these terrorist attacks though aimed at one nation wounded an entire world.[3]

The current crisis of State-to-State arms control, whether multilateral or bilateral, is also faced with this new threat. As the contribution of arms control to international security is questioned and challenged, the time has come to grasp the momentum and show cooperation beyond traditional boundaries. In the midst of grief and sorrow for lost lives one must not neglect how much worse the situation would have been if weapons of mass destruction had been used. Particular measures are needed for tactical nuclear weapons (TNWs), which are the category of nuclear weapons least regulated by States and most likely to end up in the hands of terrorists or unauthorised persons. Legally binding measures on TNWs would make an important additional contribution to combating terrorism and enhancing the overall international security environment.

For years the control of TNWs has remained an obstacle and a challenge in the United States-Russian nuclear arms control dialogue. The existing arms control and disarmament treaties, mainly the Intermediate Nuclear Forces (INF) and the Strategic Arms Reduction Treaties (START), left the difficult issue of tactical nuclear weapons unaddressed. The only regime covering this category of nuclear weapons is not legally binding and lacks crucial elements of transparency, provisions on implementation and dispute settlement mechanisms.

INTRODUCTION—THE KALININGRAD CASE

Ten years after the end of the East-West arms race, the international community is engaged in tackling the illicit trafficking of small arms, banning landmines, controlling the proliferation of missiles and now combating terrorism. The public tends to forget, however, the vast amounts of nuclear weapons still in existence—until these become a cause for concern again, that is. Over the past years TNWs have lacked attention not only in the media and among the wider public but also among those specifically addressing arms control and disarmament matters. So, why should curbing TNWs be of such importance now?

In January 2001 the international media reported alarming news about TNWs. According to United States officials, for the past year, Russia had been moving battlefield nuclear weapons to the Kaliningrad enclave on the Baltic Sea between Lithuania and Poland.[4] The President of the Russian Federation, Vladimir Putin, strongly denied the reports.[5] The controversial news and surrounding secrecy raised security concerns among the neighbouring States and calls were issued for international inspectors to visit the Kaliningrad site.[6]

Kaliningrad became the focus of concern in 2001 for many reasons. There are no legally binding treaties, which would obligate Russia to be more transparent about its TNWs or their deployment. The only existing regime covering TNWs is considered to be politically binding only and dates from 1991/1992. Regardless of the uncertainties influencing discussions over the situation in Kaliningrad, it is apparent that nuclear weapons still play a role in international politics. The current legal and political control of TNWs is inadequate and deserves more attention. A commitment to finding long-lasting measures is clearly needed. The relevant governments have an opportunity to assure the world that TNWs are safely stored and in the process of being dismantled in an appropriate way. One important aspect is also to secure the vast amount of fissile material that is the result of the nuclear weapons reductions.

This paper looks at the weaknesses associated with unilateral measures currently regulating TNWs and uses the *Kaliningrad case* to illustrate the situation. The paper analyses the uncertain status of the 1991 parallel unilateral declarations, takes a thorough look at the *Kalinigrad case* and concludes with recommending legally binding, codified measures to curb problems related to TNWs.

THE 1991 PARALLEL UNILATERAL DECLARATIONS

Tactical nuclear weapons have remained outside contractual arms control frameworks. The only existing regime regulating TNWs turned ten years old in Autumn of 2001. It consists of parallel presidential initiatives adopted by the leaders of the two largest nuclear weapon States, the United States and the Russian Federation, in 1991. At the time it came into being, the regime was considered as a bold step, and today it still represents one of the most significant nuclear weapons disarmament measures undertaken since the end of the Cold War.

However, the regime is highly vulnerable on various counts. First, its legal status is uncertain and needs to be clarified. The declarations are thought to be politically binding only. However, it is also well recognised that under international law unilateral acts in specific circumstances may create legal effects. There is no codified law on this matter and the applicable principles are quite complicated and have to be interpreted on a case-by-case basis. In this respect it is regrettable that the United States and the Russian Federation have failed to codify their promises into an international agreement or a treaty that would bring more clarity from the legal point of view and avoid the difficult task of interpreting the fine lines between politically and legally binding measures.

Second, the regime does not include any mechanisms for exchanging information or any means of verification. For example, the Russian Federation had provided an unofficial deadline for completing its pledged TNWs reductions by 2000.[7] However, as of this writing, no official statement has been made as to whether the promised reductions have been effected, or, if not, as to when they are going to be effected. It is thus of utmost importance that the TNWs regime be strengthened in order to reduce uncertainties and build confidence.

In the following, I will take a brief look at the legal and political status of the 1991 regime. It is important to note at this stage that regardless of the status of the 1991 declarations this regime is a weak one. The legal effects of these unilateral declarations do not in themselves improve the situation because it would be very difficult to bring allegations of violation to any binding international judicature. Any dispute over the regime will have to be settled by diplomatic means, which require the good will of both parties.

Unilateral Measures under International Law

The majority of unilateral acts practised by States are meant to be politically binding only. However, in certain situations the unilateral acts of States may give rise to international legal obligations.[8] This part of international law is contested and constantly challenged by States and has remained to a considerable degree unsettled. Many States view with suspicion the idea that they might be legally committed to obligations that do not necessarily take legal form. Despite this, the International Law Commission (ICL) has proposed to the General Assembly that the law of unilateral acts of States be considered as a subject for codification and progressive development.[9]

Various governments are of the view that since unilateral acts are important in day-to-day diplomatic affairs it would be useful to codify the applicable law. Clarifying legal principles related to unilateral measures would promote stability in international relations. However, at the same time some States consider that unilateral measures are useful precisely because of the freedom they afford and fear that codification could harm and constrain their use.[10]

The legal aspects of unilateral acts by States are in general complicated and sensitive. Applying these rules to defence matters and in particular to the unilateral declarations on TNWs—a regime that pertains to a particularly complex category of nuclear arms control and disarmament matters—is no doubt a challenging task. However, the growing desire for less stringent commitments in the area of international security, including arms control and disarmament, increases the need to clarify the principles governing unilateral acts. For those officials actively engaged in non-contractual measures on a daily basis this is no longer just a question of academic exercise. They need to know where they stand in terms of decision-making as well as liability. Before embarking on an era of unilateralism, States should take stock of what this actually entails both in terms of politics as well as law.

Regardless of the obviously muddy waters, I attempt below to analyse the current status of the 1991 unilateral declarations on TNWs from a legal point of view. In so doing, I use the most common international legal principles and rules applicable; however, it should be noted that the case could also be argued on other legal grounds, for example through the principle of estoppel.

The 1974 Nuclear Tests Cases

The question of legal effects of unilateral acts by States has been taken up by the ICJ on several occasions. The ICJ is the principal judicial organ of the United Nations and its judgements are referred to as the authoritative statements of international law. The most cited source with respect to the legal effects of unilateral declarations is the 1974 *Nuclear Tests Cases (Australia vs. France and New Zealand vs. France)*, which concerned French nuclear tests in the Pacific Ocean. Australia and New Zealand argued that the tests caused, *inter alia*, environmental damage to their national territories. The highest French authorities (the President, the Foreign Minister and the Defence Minister) declared on several occasions in public that France would no longer conduct nuclear tests in the Pacific. The court found that these declarations were binding undertakings by France, and that therefore the case had no object since the dispute had been removed. Despite dismissing the case, the Court had established the principles governing legal effects of unilateral acts by States.

The ICJ stated:

> It is well recognized that declarations made by way of unilateral acts, concerning legal or factual situations, may have an effect of creating legal obligations... When it is the *intention of the State* making the declaration that it should become bound according to its terms, that intention confers on the declaration the character of a legal undertaking. An undertaking of this kind, *if given publicly* and with the intention to be bound, even though not made within the context of international negotiations, is binding...
>
> Of course not all unilateral acts imply obligation; but a State may choose to take up a certain position in relation to a particular matter with the intention of being bound—*the intention is to be ascertained by interpretation of the act.*[11]

A State's intention is to be established through the usual process of interpretation. Unilateral declarations are often imprecise in language as they are given in a less stringent manner and are not debated and negotiated as a treaty text would be. The challenge lies in defining the intended meaning and scope of a given unilateral declaration. The 1969 Vienna Convention on the Law of Treaties contains well-established principles on the interpretation of treaties. These general rules are relevant also in relation to unilateral acts.

According to Article 31:

> A treaty shall be interpreted in good faith in accordance with the ordinary meaning to be given to the terms of the treaty in their context and in the light of its object and purpose.

And according to Article 32:

> Recourse may be had to supplementary means of interpretation, including the preparatory work of the treaty and the circumstances of its conclusion, in order to confirm the meaning resulting from the application of Article 31, or to determine the meaning when the interpretation according to Article 31 a) leaves the meaning ambiguous or obscure; or b) leads to a result which is manifestly absurd or unreasonable.

The relevance of Article 32 with respect to unilateral acts is narrow, as the availability of *travaux préparatoires* is often limited.

The Three Presidential Initiatives

The 1991 TNWs regime is comprised of three presidential declarations on nuclear weapons. The first declaration was articulated by President George Bush on 27 September 1991.[12] This was shortly followed on a parallel basis by a statement made by the President of the Soviet Union, Michail Gorbachev, on national television on 5 October.[13] Later, in 1992, the Soviet declaration was reconfirmed and slightly expanded by Boris Yeltsin, the then President of the Russian Federation.[14] President Bush publicly noted that the President of the Russian Federation honoured the former Soviet commitments to take comparable steps reducing TNWs.

In his 1991 declaration, President Bush committed the United States to eliminating its entire inventory of ground-launched short-range nuclear weapons (i.e., all nuclear artillery shells and short-range ballistic missile warheads), and to withdraw all TNWs from surface ships, attack submarines and land-based naval aircraft (i.e., all nuclear Tomahawk cruise missiles from ships and submarines, and all nuclear bombs aboard aircraft carriers).

President Gorbachev answered that the Soviet Union would in turn eliminate all its nuclear artillery shells, nuclear warheads for tactical missiles and nuclear mines. It would remove nuclear warheads of anti-aircraft missiles from the army and store them in central bases. He also pledged to destroy part of them. He declared that all TNWs from surface ships and multi-purpose submarines would be removed. These weapons as well as weapons from ground-based naval aircraft would be placed in central storage areas and part of them would be dismantled.

President Gorbachev also offered on a reciprocal basis to completely eliminate all TNWs from Soviet naval forces and remove nuclear bombs and missiles from tactical aircraft.

President Yeltsin added his part some months later. He reaffirmed the prior Soviet commitments while adding some new elements to the regime. Yeltsin promised that Russia would eliminate one third of its sea-based TNWs and one half of its nuclear warheads for anti-aircraft missiles and stocks of air-launched tactical nuclear munitions. The remaining air force tactical nuclear weapons could be removed to central storage facilities on the basis of reciprocity.

These three presidential initiatives were not issued in the specific legal format of international treaties. Rather, they were included as part of speeches addressing the general political situation and some particular policies with respect to TNWs and other categories of weapons. They also indicated what response was expected from the other party, although not all pledges required that they be matched. The declarations thus leave room for different interpretations. Their exact meaning and scope are unclear. The two States involved might actually have had very different views regarding the actual understanding and practical implementation of their commitments.

At the time the declarations were issued, a unilateral approach was selected due to political and military instabilities in the former Soviet Union, which lead to concerns over the safety of nuclear weapons in the Soviet Union. According to Bush's statement, bold and swift action was required instead of long treaty negotiations.[15] According to William Potter and Nikolai Sokov of the Monterey Institute Center for Non-Proliferation Studies, it was also easier to obtain the support of the United States military for a non-binding initiative than for a formal regime with verification procedures. The same authors also claim that preparations for a treaty on TNWs was in progress in the Soviet Union and that despite the non-binding Bush initiative it was still hoped by some officials in Moscow that a treaty would later be concluded.[16]

The United States decided to adopt these measures on a unilateral basis rather than through a legally binding treaty. However, as already stated, international treaties are not the only means by which a State can enter into legal obligations. A unilateral declaration is binding under international law on the State issuing it, if that State intends to be bound by it.

Current Unclear Status of the Regime

In principle, unilateral measures are politically binding only. According to the rulings of the ICJ, however, in order to define the possible legal effects of the 1991 unilateral declarations we must look at the intention given to the unilateral promises as well as to the circumstances in which they were made. The Court has held that publicly given statements are indication of intention to be bound by the act. By issuing a statement publicly, the State is bound to assume that other States are taking note of and rely on these statements.[17]

Intention to be bound

President Bush issued his statement publicly on 27 September 1991 and President Gorbachev followed within a week. The Soviet statement answered Bush's proposals and added some measures, which could have been taken on a reciprocal basis.

At the time President Bush justified his choice of unilateral action by pointing to the challenge that the fast and dramatic changes in Eastern Europe presented. He stated that "the world has changed in a fantastic pace, with each day writing a fresh page of history before yesterday's ink has even dried". He announced the measures as a promise to help Soviet society in its turn towards democracy and freedom. President Bush called for the United States to provide the inspiration for lasting peace. In the midst of these rapid developments there was no time for long treaty negotiations. The decision of form was based on the need to take prompt measures, not on the need to take non-binding measures.

According to legal principles, the intention of a State to be legally bound by its declarations cannot be automatically presumed because the guiding principle in international law is the *free will of the State*, namely the prerogative of the State to decide when and under what conditions it wants to restrict its behaviour. In order to infer the intent to be bound, the language of the declarations with regards to the obligations assumed should at the very least be clear and precise. In the case of the TNWs declarations, the language pertaining to the withdrawal and destruction of TNWs is quite clear, however, other details such as the implementation of the announced measures remain unspecified.

It is also worth noting that the Soviet Union registered its declaration as an official document of the General Assembly and as an official document of the Security Council.[18] This indicates willingness to formalise the act. However, the United States did not register its declaration.

Good Faith—Right to Rely

Sometimes unilateral acts are not only binding to the extent that the declaring State intends them to be, but also as far as they create expectations. Therefore, some unilateral measures are binding irrespective of the intention of the State undertaking them.

In this respect it is noteworthy that the measures President Bush announced were not meant to be purely unilateral but rather were expected to be reciprocated at least to some extent by the Soviet Union. As Bush put it, the measures were to be taken "some on our own, some on their own, some together". This points to the principle of international law whereby the other party has the *right to rely* on the good faith of the declaring State and expect that the measures announced be carried out in practice. The Soviet Union gave similar directives as the United States and made significant changes to its defence structures. President Gorbachev stated that the Soviet Union was taking these steps *in response* and on a *reciprocal basis*. Under these circumstances the Soviet Union has the *right to rely* on the 1991 regime formed by the parallel unilateral declarations. And, vice versa, the United States is entitled to rely on the statement made by President Gorbachev.

These measures, which represent one of the largest nuclear disarmament commitments ever undertaken, were noted by the world at large. In particular their implementation was noted in Europe where the United States had deployed large numbers of TNWs. Both the United States and the Soviet Union were equally bound to suppose that other States would take note of these declarations and have the right to rely on expectations that the two countries respect their respective declarations.

The subsequent behaviour of the United States and Russia gives guidance to other States when interpreting the status of the 1991 declarations. Both the United States and the Russian Federation have provided information on the implementation of the 1991 regime. This has taken place mainly through the Non-Proliferation Treaty (NPT) process in their respective statements on nuclear disarmament. Even though the information available is not precise as to numbers or other details, it is still sufficient for other States to assume that the declarations are still respected by the United States and the Russian Federation and to rely on them.

It is difficult to identify any one single factor that would be decisive in interpreting the current status of the 1991 TNWs regime. However, there certainly are various aspects that need to be carefully considered before judging whether these declarations are actually legally binding on the issuing States. As we have seen, at least enough evidence exists to make it difficult to automatically presume that the declarations are politically binding only.

Beyond the legal considerations raised above, there of course remains the larger question of whether States have confidence in the current situation regarding TNWs. In this respect the *Kalinigrad case* to which I turn next illustrates the difficulties involved.

THE KALININGRAD CASE IN THE MEDIA

Media reports in January 2001about the possible movement of TNWs to Kaliningrad came as a shock. It was an exciting story for the media: secret weapons and uncertain motives, revealed to the public by unidentified secret service sources in the United States and denied by the highest authorities in the Russian Federation. The international media covered the Kaliningrad story for several days until the outbreak of foot and mouth disease in Europe shifted focus elsewhere. However, the news reporting served as an alarm bell and a wake up call for policy makers about an issue that for long had been lacking attention.

In an article in the *Washington Post* on 4 January 2001, Pentagon spokesman Kenneth Bacon declined to confirm the intelligence report. However, he stated that "if the Russians were placing TNWs in Kaliningrad, it would violate their pledge that they were removing nuclear weapons from the Baltics and that the Baltics should be nuclear-free".[19]

The article immediately raised international security concerns. During the same day the Russian Ministry of Defence denied the information contained in the article. According to the Ministry's statement, the *Washington Post* article "does not conform with reality" and Russia's tactical nuclear warheads are at their "permanent stationing sites and have not been transferred anywhere". The spokesman of the Baltic Fleet Capt. Anatoly Lobsky stated that "the Baltic Sea is a nuclear-weapon-free zone, and Russia's Baltic Fleet scrupulously observes its international commitments".[20] He also commented that the American report "can only be a political provocation".[21] An even stronger denial was issued two days later by President Vladimir Putin himself who was quoted by the Interfax news agency as stating that the allegations were "rubbish".[22]

Despite the statements and assurances given by Russian officials, the neighbouring States expressed concern. It was uncertain what Russia considered as the specific scope of "its international commitments". Particularly given the nature of the 1991 regime it is difficult to know whether the United States and Russia even have the same understanding of their respective commitments, as the regime lacks common guidelines on implementation. Poland stated that it wanted to discuss the Kaliningrad issue with its NATO allies and called for an international verification team to be sent to Kaliningrad.[23] The Polish Defense Minister Bronislaw Komorowski said the government was taking the issue very seriously.[24] Lithuania was more cautious and its Foreign Minister Antanas Valionis said that the report was not confirmed and that "similar reports have been appearing several times a year but after raising public concern they after some time are usually forgotten".[25]

The United States Department of State spokesman Richard Boucher admitted that there were some concerns and said the issue would be taken up with the Russians.[26] It was reported later in January that then-Secretary of State Madeleine Albright did not receive a detailed response from Russian Foreign Minister Igor Ivanov while taking the issue up with him in discussions.[27] According to unidentified United States officials, the Russian government had replied to a formal diplomatic note sent by the Department of State that there were no nuclear arms in Kaliningrad.[28]

After a few days the media reporting on Kaliningrad came to a halt. The controversial story left questions unanswered for the wider public, however.

In February 2001, after over a month of absence, Kaliningrad suddenly came back to the headlines. Information from satellite images was revealed as the source of evidence that Russia had been moving TNWs to Kaliningrad. The reporting came once more through journalist Bill Gertz of the *Washington Times*. The latter claimed that the satellite photographs showed the transfer of nuclear weapons from mainland Russia to the enclave of Kaliningrad. First the weapons had been spotted aboard a military train at a seaport near St Petersburg and later satellites had detected their arrival in Kaliningrad. It was also reported that concerns over TNWs deployments in Kaliningrad dated back to 1998.[29]

Later it was revealed that Norwegian military sources were also aware of the transfer of TNWs to Kaliningrad. A Norwegian Defence Department official said that the weapons were aimed at targets in Europe and Scandinavia and could not reach the United States. The Norwegian Foreign Ministry did not confirm the report and declared that Norway was unaware of any TNW deployments in Kaliningrad.[30]

The Unanswered Questions

The *Kaliningrad case* shows how politically vulnerable Europe is with respect to TNWs. Controversial and incomplete information clearly breeds suspicions that need to be addressed and clarified. The European Union is rapidly developing its security identity. The transparency gap with respect to TNWs is enormous compared to the level of trust achieved vis-à-vis other categories of weapons in Europe such as for instance conventional weapons. Under current political and economic circumstances it should not be impossible to address the question of TNWs—in fact, should this matter finally be settled it would positively affect general security conditions in Europe and enhance cooperation at various levels.

New or Stored Weapons?

There are no codified obligations that would prevent Russia from deploying or storing TNWs wherever it wants on its own territory. However, States are not bound by legal obligations alone; political, economic and military implications of State action matter. Despite presuming the lack of legally binding obligations in the *Kaliningrad case* (if the allegations were actually true) it makes a difference whether Russia had stored TNWs in Kaliningrad or whether it was re-stationing TNWs there.

The Russian Navy has been requesting permission to return non-strategic nuclear weapons to surface ships and submarines, which would unravel the existing TNWs regime. In addition, there is a greater general reliance on nuclear weapons in Russia's defence strategy. According to Nikolai Sokov, the *Kaliningrad case* deserves attention regardless of whether it has been accurately reported in the *Washington Post* article by Bill Gertz. Sokov states that within the strategic concept adopted by Russia it would make sense to pre-deploy TNWs secretly in Kaliningrad. The strategic concept foresees the limited use of nuclear weapons in order to increase the cost of conflict to the attacker and bring about the early termination of hostilities.[31]

The Russian statements did not clarify whether nuclear weapons have been stored in Kaliningrad over a longer period of time. If Kaliningrad has a "central storage site" as per the 1991 unilateral declaration, the weapons could be stored there permanently, in accordance with Russia's commitments. Kaliningrad is a strong military outpost. It has previously served as an important transit route, and therefore probably has the requisite facilities to host warheads.

In a press conference in March 2001 prior to President Vladimir Putin's visit to Sweden, Stefan Noreen, the Swedish government's top official on Russian affairs, said that Sweden could not rule out the presence of nuclear weapons in Kaliningrad. The weapons could be in transit from locations in Moscow's former Eastern European satellites. He intimated that the Russian denials related to the further deployment and build-up of TNWs rather than to the prior existence of such weapons in Kaliningrad.[32] According to William Potter, this assumption is contrary to the generally held belief that all TNWs previously stationed in Eastern Europe had been returned to Russia by 1992.[33]

The re-deployment of TNWs would be an alarming development for the European security environment. Russian officials have previously identified the deployment of TNWs near the borders of NATO countries as a countermeasure to NATO's eastward enlargement.[34] After the events of 11 September 2001, it could be expected that in the future NATO-Russian cooperation should improve rather than deteriorate.[35] Greater cooperation under the Founding Act in the fight against terrorism could open new possibilities for reviving discussions on weapons of mass-destruction (WMD) in general and transparency on TNWs in particular.

Why Revealed to the Media? Timing? Political Weapons?

When Bill Gertz's article appeared in the media, many asked themselves why the information had been revealed and what was the relevance of timing? Once Kaliningrad became the focus of international attention, it raised more questions than official sources answered. The

Americans revealed, the Russians denied. In the middle, the Europeans were trying to hold economic talks. The burden of proof over the *Kaliningrad case* does not seem to lie with either Russia or the United States.

The news was based on information leaked by United States intelligence sources on the strength of satellite photographs. Currently Europe relies heavily on American satellite intelligence, which is more developed than European capabilities in the area. However, it is, of course, possible to gather independent information through commercial satellite imageries as well as inspection visits under other treaty regimes and arrangements (e.g. the Conventional Forces in Europe (CFE) Treaty, the 1999 Vienna Document, the Open Skies Treaty). It was reported that the Norwegian defence officials had seen the evidence. As a NATO member, Norway is in a different position from that of those neighbouring countries that do not have access to NATO infrastructure.

On the same day that Bill Gertz published the second report, Sweden, which was holding the presidency of the European Union, was discussing with Russia the expansion of the European Union and the future of Kaliningrad. The original purpose of the meeting was to work out a development plan for Russia's Baltic enclave. There are worries that the economic gap between Kaliningrad and its neighbours will grow and cause instability in the region as the enclave could become surrounded by European Union members in the near future. However, the concerns over the Russian missiles added yet another serious factor to the list of problems already associated with the enclave: organised crime, smuggling and trafficking, high rates of HIV/AIDS and tuberculosis.[36]

During the day the European Union received top-level assurances that no nuclear weapons were deployed in Kaliningrad. According to the Governor of Kaliningrad Vladimir Yegorov, the *Kaliningrad case* was an attempt to disrupt cooperation between the Russian Federation and the European Union.[37]

Verification Inspection

International inspection to verify a specific site requires a negotiated agreement. Within the existing treaties such as CFE, INF and START, inspections are part of the comprehensive verification regime, which specifies in great detail the scope of inspections as well as their rules of procedure. The inspection of a military base is considered to be one of the most intrusive means of verification.

Following the reports of the movement of TNWs to Kaliningrad, a call was issued for the international verification of the enclave. The 1991 regime on TNWs does not contain any agreed mechanisms for the inspection of TNWs facilities. Military inspections of Kaliningrad have been conducted under the auspices of other treaty regimes. Obviously the inspectors should restrict their work to the mandate of their inspection within the scope of the treaty regime. However, it is likely that unofficially inspectors gather information related to nuclear weapons—i.e., whether the security arrangements in the area match the level of security expected for nuclear warheads.

It is highly unlikely that the Russians would allow an international inspection focusing on TNWs in Kaliningrad. Vladimir Kozin, a senior counsel for the Russian Foreign Ministry, suggests in his article in the *Moscow Times* that if the countries of the region are concerned about the issue, then mechanisms must be developed for inspections. This would entail mutual nuclear inspections on the territories of NATO countries and those countries of the region that are not currently NATO members.[38]

Where are the NATO Nuclear Weapons?

The United States has been more open about its European deployments of TNWs. However, greater transparency is needed still. On occasions the host States have not been informed about the existence and movements of nuclear weapons on their territory. It is also uncertain what proportion of the wider public is even aware that their country hosts these weapons. The policies of the host countries could change radically if the policy makers where faced with strong domestic pressure against hosting TNWs on national soil.

Germany is one of the European States where American air-delivered TNWs are deployed. The German air force currently has the capability to deliver these weapons. However, according to some reports Germany might give up this option in the future. According to Otfried Nassauer, if Germany gave up its ability to deliver American nuclear bombs, it could increase the likelihood that the rest of the United States nuclear bombs in Europe might finally be withdrawn. At the same time there have been reports that the United States has withdrawn its nuclear weapons from

Greece.[39] It is unclear whether this was carried out as part of replacing older nuclear weapons with new ones or if the purpose was to withdraw American weapons permanently from Greece. The latter would reduce the number of host countries to six: Belgium, Germany, Italy, Netherlands, Turkey and the United Kingdom.[40]

In his article in this compilation, Vladimir Kozin, a senior counsellor of the Russian Foreign Ministry, writing in his personal capacity, states that it would not be beyond the realm of possibility to reach a global ban on TNWs, analogous to the INF. This would settle the question of TNWs once and for all, just as the INF did for intermediate-range nuclear weapons. The INF serves as a precedent in many ways. At the time it was concluded many doubted that a complete ban was achievable, however, due to various events it came true regardless of the claims that the original zero-proposal by President Ronald Reagan was meant as a bluff.

Russia might prefer to discuss the question of TNWs in a broader European context. There are at least two incentives, which are often identified as possible means of persuading Russian to discuss TNWs: (1) codification of the non-binding pledge by NATO not to deploy nuclear weapons on the territories of the new member States, and (2) the withdrawal of American TNWs from Europe altogether. However, these are generally viewed as sensitive and complicated issues for NATO to take up. The future course of relations between the Russian Federation and NATO will needless to say have a tremendous impact on the question of TNWs.

CONCLUDING REMARKS—HOW TO TACKLE UNILATERALISM?

With respect to unilateralism, the *Kaliningrad case* serves as an example of what to expect from unilateral measures. States are more unlikely to volunteer information related to defence matters than under a binding obligation to do so. It is obvious and understandable, that countries within the range of these weapons are worried. In the words of Polish Defence Minister, "the problem is whether we can treat assurances that there are no nuclear weapons in Kaliningrad as credible".[41]

A prerequisite for accepting the given assurances would be a high level of mutual trust between States. This, however, would require transparency and an adequate degree of openness regarding the status of TNWs and their intended role. At present the international community does not even know how many thousands of these weapons are still in existence, let alone details on their deployment, storage or destruction. At the same time it is apparent that the Russian Federation is relying more heavily on its nuclear arsenal to provide for its national security.

On the other hand, the United States has taken a new unilateral approach to international affairs. This has raised legitimate concerns about how international security structures and State relations will be affected over the long run. Many States have expressed their concern over the deterioration of arms control regimes. This reflects the broader problem of crumbling trust in international law. At the time of this writing, the United States is engaged in the process of conducting a comprehensive Defence Review. This will provide major clues as to the future of international security structures. Some information that has been leaked to the public suggests that the United States is interested in the development of a new generation of "more usable" TNWs.

Reaffirmation to the 1991 Regime

In this paper I have analysed the difficulties associated with unilateral measures under international law, in particular the weaknesses and unclear status of the 1991 unilateral declarations regulating TNWs. In this respect I introduced the *Kalinigrad case* in order to illustrate the current uncertainties and obstacles hindering attempts to enhance transparency with respect to the status of TNWs in Europe. The aim was to argue that as a priority clear indications are needed from the United States and the Russian Federation of their commitment to the 1991 unilateral regime. Political pressure from other States in this regard has grown during the recent years, for example this is apparent from the increased number of statements within the NPT process as well at the United Nations First Committee. Ultimately, however, it is the Russian Federation and the United States, the owners of these weapons, which need to take the necessary concrete steps.

There is a broad range of measures the two States could adopt in order to assure the world that a stable disarmament process is taking place with regards to TNWs in Europe. Such measures could include assurances of stockpile security, increased transparency on the destruction of TNWs already completed through a reporting mechanism, introduction of verification measures to assure and demonstrate compliance, a moratorium on the development of a new generation of TNWs, as well as the adoption of further reductions.

One of the priority measures should be the reiteration of a clear commitment to the 1991 regime. The traditional type of disarmament and arms control treaties—"heavy hundreds of pages of START Treaties"—are not the only means to commit to legally binding and effective instruments. A less stringent regime could be established by adopting precise parallel instruments recommitting to the declarations and adding some general, broad guidelines on implementation. This, in turn, would pave the way for establishing a comprehensive database on TNWs in the future. Recommitment could be adopted in a Memorandum of Understanding. Gradually the commitments should be transformed into a binding international treaty by codifying the already achieved limitations and reductions.

The international community needs to be reassured that progress is being made in controlling this category of nuclear weapons. It should be assured that TNWs waiting to be dismantled are stored safely and that their destruction is proceeding as planned. It is high time that the rumours about the deployment or re-deployment of tactical nuclear weapons in Europe are halted. This is of concern not only to the security policy makers but also to the wider public in general

Endnotes

1. The writer is a visiting fellow at the United Nations Institute for Disarmament Research (UNIDIR) in Geneva and in charge of the Tactical Nuclear Weapons project. This paper is based on a study prepared for UNIDIR on the political and legal aspects of the 1991 Parallel Unilateral Declarations. The study was made possible by a contribution from the Government of Finland.
2. NATO Press release 124, 12 September 2001. On line at http://www.nato.int/docu/pr/2001/p01-124e.htm.
3. Kofi Annan, "Fighting Terrorism on a Global Front", *The New York Times*, 21 September 2001.
4. Bill Gertz, "Russia Transfers Nuclear Arms to Baltics", *The Washington Times*, 3 January 2001.

5. "Putin Denies Missile Movements", *BBC News Europe*, 6 January 2001.
6. "Poland concern over Russia missiles" and "Russian Reports Worry Poland and Lithuania", *BBC News Europe*, 4 January 2001.
7. William M. Arkin, Robert S. Norris and Joshua Handler, "Taking Stock. Worldwide Nuclear Deployments 1998", NRDC Nuclear Program. The report can be downloaded from http://www.nrdc.org/nuclear/tkstock/download.asp.
8. Of the international legal obligations of unilateral acts see for instance Ian Brownlie, *Principles of Public International Law*, Oxford: Clarendon Press, 1979.
9. Reports of the ILC are obtainable on line at http://www.un.org/law/ilc/reports.
10. A related interesting debate on the legally binding character of treaties, Memorandum of understandings and unilateral acts can be found for example between Jan Klabbers, *The Concept of Treaty in International Law*, The Hague: Kluwer Law International, 1996 and Anthony Aust, *Modern Treaty Law and Practice*, Cambridge: Cambridge University Press, 2000.
11. *Nuclear Tests Cases*, ICJ Reports 1974, 253, 267, paragraphs 42ff; 457, 45ff. There were two cases: Australia vs. France and New Zealand vs. France. With respect to the matter discussed here the two judgments are identical. Emphasis added by author.
12. Unilateral Declaration by the President of the United States of America, 27 September 1991 (Bush's statement). Obtainable on line at http://bushlibrary.tamu.edu/papers/1991/91092704.html and titled "Address to the Nation on Reducing United States and Soviet Nuclear Weapons".
13. Unilateral Declaration by the President of the Union of the Soviet Socialist Republic (Gorbachev's statement), 5 October 1991. Letter dated 11 October 1991 from the Permanent Representative of the Union of the Soviet Socialist Republic to the United Nations addressed to the Secretary-General, A/46/592, 23 October 1991.
14. Unilateral Declaration by the President of the Russian Federation (Yeltsin's statement), 29 January 1992. Bush's statement.
15. Ibid.
16. William Potter et al., *Tactical Nuclear Weapons. Options for Control*, UNIDIR, Geneva: United Nations, 2000, pp. 8-9.
17. *Nuclear Tests Case (Australia vs. France)*, ICJ Reports 1974, pp. 253, 267-268.

18. A/46/592. S/23161, 23 October 1991.
19. Bill Gertz, "Russia Transfers Nuclear Arms to Baltics", *The Washington Times*, 3 January 2001.
20. Walter Pincus, "Russia Moving Warheads", *Washington Post*, 4 January 2001.
21. "US Fears over Russia 'Missiles on Move'", *BBC News*, 4 January 2001.
22. "Putin Denies Missile Movemetns", *BBC News*, 6 January 2001.
23. "Russian Reports Worry Poland and Lithuania", *BBC News*, 4 January 2001.
24. "Poland Concern over Russia Missiles", *BBC News*, 4 January 2001.
25. "US Fears over Russia 'Missiles on Move'", *BBC News*, 4 January 2001.
26. Ibid.
27. "US Raises Kaliningrad Nuclear Reports with Russia", http://www.russiatoday.com/news.php3?id=253380&section=default. Reported in Nuclear Policy Project FLASH, Vol. 3, No. 3, 22 January 2001. The European Union also took the issue up in talks regarding the European Union's expansion and the future of Kaliningrad.
28. Bill Gertz, "Satellites Pinpoint Russian Nuclear Arms in Baltics", *The Washington Times*, 15 February 2001.
29. Bill Gertz, "Satellites Pinpoint Russian Nuclear Arms in Baltics", *The Washington Times*, 15 February 2001.
30. "Russia Poses New Atomic Threat" translated from the original Norwegian script on the internet pages of the *Aftonposten*, http://www.aftonposten.no, 7 March 2001.
31. Nikolai Sokov, "The 'Tactical Nuclear Scare' of 2001", CNS Reports, http//cns.miis.edu/pubs/reports/tnw.htm.
32. "Sweden Can't Rule out Nuclear Arms in Kaliningrad", *Reuters Stockholm*, 6 March 2001.
33. William C. Potter, Monterey Institute Center for Non-Proliferation Studies, interview at the Palais des Nations, Geneva, 26 July 2001.
34. The former Secretary of Defense William S. Cohen remarked in January 2001 that Russia was going to be a major challenge to the new United States administration and specified tactical nuclear weapons as a cause for concern. National Press Club Newsmakers Luncheon, Washington DC, http://www.defenselink.mil/speeches/2001/s20010110-secdef.html, 1 January 2001.
35. Press Statement of the Meeting in extraordinary session of the NATO-Russia Permanent Joint Council at Ambassadorial level, 13 September 2001. On line at http://www.nato.int/docu/pr/2001/p010913e/htm.

36. Barry James, "Nuclear Arms in a Russian Enclave? EU Questions Kremlin", *International Herald Tribune*, 16 February 2001.
37. "EU Gets Assurances on Nukes in Kaliningrad", *Reuters*, 15 February 2001.
38. Vladimir Kozin, "Who Really Wants Baltic Nukes", *The Moscow Times*, 26 February 2001.
39. "US Nuclear Weapons in Greece Removed", http://athensnews.dolnet.gr/athweb/nathens.print_unique?e=C&f=12854&m=A01&aa=2&eidos=S, sited in the NFP Weekly (Nuclear Policy Project Flash), Vol. 3, No. 4, 29 January 2001.
40. William M. Arkin, Robert S. Norris and Joshua Handler, "Taking Stock. Worldwide Nuclear Deployments 1998", NRDC Nuclear Program, p. 18.
41. "Poland Concern over Russia Missiles", *BBC News*, 4 January 2001.

CHAPTER 9

TACTICAL NUCLEAR WEAPONS REGIME: IS IT LEGALLY BINDING?

Sergey Radchenko

Unilateralism, the latest fad in the arms control process between Russia and the United States raises doubts in the minds of many informed observers. Disarmament experts often mistrust unilateral cuts in nuclear arsenals, partly because such reductions are not considered to be legally binding, and are hence easily reversible, which presumably would not be the case with a treaty-like arrangement. Yet few experts take a close look at the legal consequences of unilateral disarmament in the context of international law, and presumptions as to the legal status of unilateral arms reductions continue to exist even in the absence of in-depth analysis. The purpose of this chapter is not necessarily to disprove these presumptions, but to examine the legal issues involved, filling the interdisciplinary gap, as it were. The chapter considers the current tactical nuclear weapons (TNWs) "regime". formed by the unilateral declarations on reductions of tactical nuclear weapons issued by the Presidents of the United States and the Soviet Union/Russia in 1991/92.

On 27 September 1991, President Bush, eager to address the issue of TNWs without going through lengthy discussions with the Soviet Union, issued a unilateral declaration, in which the United States pledged to eliminate all of its ground-launched short-range nuclear weapons (i.e., nuclear artillery shells and short-range ballistic missile warheads), and withdraw all TNWs from surface ships and attack submarines, as well as from land-based naval aircraft. Days later, Soviet President Gorbachev announced that the USSR would in response eliminate all nuclear artillery shells, nuclear warheads for tactical missiles and nuclear mines, while nuclear warheads for anti-aircraft missiles and the TNWs deployed on multipurpose submarines, surface ships and ground-based tactical aircraft would be removed to central storage facilities and partly destroyed. Gorbachev's statement also called on the United States to "completely eliminate" all TNWs from its naval forces and remove nuclear bombs and missiles from tactical aircraft, on the basis of reciprocity. On 29 January 1992, Russian President Yeltsin expanded on Gorbachev's initiative by pledging to eliminate one-third of Russia's sea-based TNWs, half of all the nuclear warheads of anti-aircraft missiles, and half of the tactical nuclear ammunition of the Air Force. He also proposed to withdraw the remaining TNWs from tactical aircraft on the basis of reciprocity with the United States.

These three declarations form a tactical nuclear weapons "regime", which has been in existence for over ten years. The central question addressed here is whether this regime is in fact legally binding, which is properly a question of international law.

The legal issue is a complicated one, and calls for three conceptually different approaches. On the one hand, it is possible that the three unilateral declarations are not strictly speaking unilateral, but that taken together they form a contractual framework of offer and acceptance, calling for the appropriate application of treaty law. On the other hand, the declarations may be strictly unilateral and binding or non-binding on the declarants in accordance with their intention. Finally, the legal force of some unilateral declarations may lie not in themselves or in the intention of their authors, but in the reliance in good faith on these declarations by third States to their detriment or to the benefit of the declarant State, which brings into play the doctrine of estoppel.

However, before considering each of these conceptual approaches, let us take a close look at how to interpret the three declarations. Although interpretation of unilateral declarations is a grey area under international law, rules of treaty interpretation provide a useful point of reference. As stipulated in Article 31 of the 1969 Vienna Convention on the Law of Treaties:

> A treaty shall be interpreted in good faith in accordance with the ordinary meaning to be given to the terms of the treaty in their context and in the light of its object and purpose.

Under Article 32:

> Recourse may be had to supplementary means of interpretation, including the preparatory work of the treaty and the circumstances of its conclusion, in order to confirm the meaning resulting from the application of article 31, or to determine the meaning when the interpretation according to article 31:
> a) leaves the meaning ambiguous or obscure ; or
> b) leads to a result which is manifestly absurd or unreasonable.

While, perhaps, the provisions of the Vienna Convention cannot be applied fully to unilateral acts of States, there is good reason to hold the principles articulated in articles 31 and 32 of the Convention as relevant to the interpretation of unilateral declarations. The practice of international tribunals supports this view. For example, in the *Laguna del Deserto* case between Chile and Argentina, the International Court of Justice (ICJ) held that under international law, similar rules of interpretation apply to treaties, unilateral acts, arbitral awards and resolutions of international organisations—that is, rules "dictated by the natural and ordinary meaning of words [with] reference to context and effectiveness".[1]

The reference to good faith in Article 31 is particularly relevant to the interpretation of unilateral acts. As the Special Rapporteur to the International Law Commission (ILC) Victor Rodriguez Cedeno pointed out:

> An act which is unilaterally formulated by a State must be interpreted in good faith, that is, in accordance with what the author State really intended to say. The task of the interpreter is precisely to identify the intentions of the parties or, in this context, of the State which unilaterally formulates the act.[2]

As regards the supplementary means of interpretation, established by article 32, these may be restrictively applied to the interpretation of unilateral acts, when the State's intentions remain unclear after the application of interpretation rules of article 31 or if such interpretation has led to absurd or unreasonable results. In this case, preparatory work may be resorted to, including internal memoranda of the State making the declaration. Of course, as the Special Rapporteur observed, such documentation may not be easily available, and even if it is, it should not be heavily relied upon. As the Arbitral Tribunal in the *Eritrea-Yemen* case stated:

> The Tribunal has been mindful that these internal memoranda do not necessarily represent the view or the policy of any Government and may be no more than the personal view that one civil servant felt moved to express to another particular civil servant at that moment.[3]

At any rate, supplementary means of interpretation may not be necessary when the meaning of the declaration or the intention of the declarant State are clear and unambiguous. As the ICJ held in the *Ambatielos* case, "where ... the text to be interpreted is clear, there is no occasion to resort to preparatory work".[4]

Finally, the notion of State consent under international law calls for the restrictive interpretation of unilateral declarations. As the ICJ ruled in the landmark *Lotus* case, "restrictions upon the independence of States cannot ... be presumed".[5]

Let us, then, move on to the TNWs declarations, keeping in mind the relevant rules of interpretation. The first conceptual approach suggests that the three unilateral declarations are not autonomous, but form something in the nature of an international agreement between the United States and the Soviet Union/Russia, falling within the scope of treaty law. Sir Gerald Fitzmaurice categorised this type of declarations as "unilateral in form, but ... contractual in substance".[6] This may happen, he argued, when the declaration in question is:

> One of two or more similar Declarations intended to be interdependent or interlocking, or [when it] is linked to the action of another State, which either forms the *quid pro quo* for it, or in respect of which it is itself the *quid pro quo*. Such a situation gives rise to a 'treaty position' in which the text or texts concerned will clearly fall to be interpreted according to the normal rules of treaty interpretation.[7]

One example of this is the type of declarations issued by States under the Optional Clause system, conferring jurisdiction to the ICJ. As Fitzmaurice points out, "the interlocking and hence basically contractual nature of these Declarations arises directly from the condition of reciprocity attached to nearly all of them".[8] In the present case, President Bush, after discussing the United States TNWs reductions, mentions that *"in turn*, I have asked the Soviets to go down this road with us" and later "again, there is every reason for the Soviet Union to match our actions".[9] Finally, Bush declared that "we *expect* our bold initiatives to meet with equally bold steps on the Soviet side".[10] President Bush's statement seems to contain in it an element of offer, and President Gorbachev's reply certainly implies acceptance of the offer: the Soviet statement refers to "the steps we are taking and the proposals we are making *in response*", and goes on to say that "the Soviet Union and the United States are taking radical measures on a reciprocal basis leading to elimination of tactical nuclear weapons".[11] Now, it is evident that the United States and the Soviet statements are not identical; that the Soviet declaration goes further and proposes deeper reductions on condition of reciprocity, while Yeltsin's statement, building on Gorbachev's initiative, calls for further steps still, again on condition of reciprocity. The United States, however, chose not to take up the Russian offer, which creates uncertainty as to the scope of the alleged treaty relationship: does it or does it not cover the Soviet and Russian initiatives unreciprocated by the United States? In deciding on its jurisdiction in the *Iranian Oil* case, the Court considered the British and Iranian declarations under the Optional Clause to find that:

> By these Declarations, jurisdiction is conferred on the Court only to the extent to which the two Declarations coincide in conferring it. As the Iranian Declaration is more limited in scope than the United Kingdom Declaration, it is the Iranian Declaration on which the Court must base itself. This is common ground between the parties.[12]

Following the Court's logic, the three TNW declarations may be regarded as constituting a legally binding agreement, leaving out the Soviet and Russian proposals, unanswered by the United States.

At the same time, there are solid arguments against viewing the three declarations as forming a treaty. One of the profound principles of treaty law is that States must intend to enter into a treaty relationship. On the part of the United States, at least, this is evidently not the case. The American declaration was made precisely out of desire to avoid protracted negotiations leading up to the conclusion of a formal treaty, such as the Strategic Arms Reduction Treaty (START), and out of recognition that, as Bush pointed out, political instability in the USSR "demand[ed] swifter, bolder action".[13]

According to the second conceptual approach, unilateral declarations are legally binding under customary international law if certain conditions are satisfied. Speaking of a declaration unilateral both in form and in substance, Fitzmaurice asserted that it:

> ... may or may not create binding legal obligations for the declaring party, according to its wording and intent, and the circumstances of its making; but it seems fairly well settled that it can and will do so if clearly intended to have that effect, and held out, so to speak, as an instrument on which others may rely and under which the declarant purports to assume such obligations.[14]

Prima facie, State practice and *opinio juris* are inconclusive. As Israel suggested to the ILC, "the vast majority of unilateral acts of States are political in nature [and] may involve obligations at the moral or political level, but they are not regulated by international law".[15] Although unilateral statements are sometimes recognised as having legal effects, it is frequently so by virtue of circumstances extraneous to the act itself, as from the negotiating context, reaction of other States, or pre-existing obligations. The Austrian Declaration of Neutrality of 25 October 1955, ostensibly a unilateral declaration, is internationally recognised as binding not merely on the basis of intent by Austria, but in the context of the Four Power negotiations and in light of recognition of the Declaration by other States. In 1946 and 1947 South Africa made a number of declarations concerning its continuing responsibilities for Namibia, as arranged under the League of Nations mandate. Judge Jessup in his separate opinion in the *South West Africa* case, expressed the view that these declarations were "an undertaking of international character by which the Union of South Africa assumed an international obligation".[16] In the opinion of other jurists, however, the South African declaration related to pre-existing obligations under the mandates system, from where it derived its legal effect. Another often-cited example of a unilateral legal statement was the Egyptian Declaration on the Suez Canal, which states, *inter alia*, that the "this Declaration, with the obligations therein, constitutes an international instrument and will be deposited and registered with the Secretariat of the United Nations".[17] Egypt, of course, intended the declaration to have a legal effect; although a number of States did not recognise it as a legal instrument.

Recently, unilateral declarations once again sparked an international controversy when in the context of the Conference on Disarmament (CD) the nuclear States—China, France, the Russian Federation, the United Kingdom and the United States—presented assurances, known as negative security guarantees, by which they undertook not to use nuclear weapons against non-nuclear-weapon States party to the Non-Proliferation Treaty (NPT). The non-aligned States, however, claimed that these guarantees were not legally binding, and insisted on a treaty-like arrangement to "codify" them.

On the other hand, there arguably exists an *opinio juris* to the effect that States, in the free exercise of their sovereignty, may bind themselves by means of strictly unilateral declarations if they so intend. A number of States recently replied to a special questionnaire, circulated by the ILC when the latter considered the subject of unilateral acts. Among others, Italy indicated that a unilateral act creates legal obligations only "if the State which made it really had the intention of obligating itself by this means".[18] Israel suggested that a State must have "expressed its intention to be regarded as legally bound".[19] Sweden, likewise, emphasised that "a unilateral act binds the enacting State, through its expressed intention to become bound".[20] El Salvador pointed out that it "attaches full importance to its own unilateral acts, in the sense of considering itself bound by the terms of any unilateral act emanating from it".[21] The submissions of these States coincide in the opinion that a unilateral act creates legal obligations only when the author States intended such an effect. Undertakings of this nature, of course, must not be in contradiction with peremptory norms of international law. The evidence presented above would hardly suffice to convince a sceptical lawyer that unilateral declarations are binding under customary international law, much less to pass a verdict on the legal nature of the TNWs regime. To help us clear up the theoretical part, let us now turn to the decisions of the ICJ.

The ICJ and its precursor, the Permanent Court of International Justice (PCIJ), have on occasion considered the question of the legal effects of unilateral declarations. The relevant judgements are both well-known and convincing. In the 1933 *Eastern Greenland* case, the Court ruled that an assurance given by the Foreign Minister of Norway to his Danish counterpart to the effect that Denmark's territorial claims in Greenland "would meet with no difficulty on the part of Norway" was legally binding, and Norway's later pretensions were deemed "unlawful and invalid". On a number of occasions the ICJ found that unilateral declarations issued by States did not have a binding character. In the case concerning *Military and Paramilitary Activities in and against Nicaragua*, the Court considered a unilateral declaration by the Junta of National Reconstruction of Nicaragua, but found nothing "from which it can be inferred that any legal undertaking was intended to exist".[22] In the *Frontier Dispute* case between Burkina Faso and Mali, the Court reiterated that "it all depends on the intention of State in question" and went on to find that a statement by the President of Mali did not satisfy this criterion.[23] The latter two rulings appeared years after the landmark judgement in the 1974 *Nuclear Tests* cases, suggesting that the view adopted by the ICJ in 1974 has since been confirmed as a valid interpretation of existing international law.

The 1974 cases concerned French nuclear tests in the Pacific Ocean, thought by the applicants, Australia and New Zealand to cause, *inter alia*, environmental damage to their respective national territories. At the time, the French President, Foreign Minister and Defence Minister in different contexts declared that the current series of French nuclear tests in the Pacific would be the last one. Contrary to the pleadings of the applicant States, the Court found that these declarations were binding undertakings by France. The Court ruled:

> When it is the intention of the State making the declaration that it should become bound according to its terms, that intention confers on the declaration the character of a legal undertaking, the State being thenceforth legally required to follow a course of conduct consistent with the declaration. An undertaking of this kind, if given publicly and with an intent to be bound, even though not made within the context of international negotiations, is binding. In these circumstances, nothing in the nature of a *quid pro quo* nor any subsequent acceptance of the declaration nor even any reply or reaction from other States, is required for the declaration to take effect.[24]

Interestingly, in the passage above the Court referred not only to the intention of the State, but to the requirement that the declaration be formulated publicly. The issue was considered at length by the ICL, and the majority thought that publicity in itself was not necessary; what is necessary is that the declaration be made known to the addressee. In the present case, the distinction does not really matter. All three TNWs declarations were publicly televised, and they pass with flying colours the test of publicity proposed by the ICJ, certainly overtaking the French declarations in the *Nuclear Tests* case, some of which were nothing more than press conference remarks.

On the other hand, the requirement of intention presents serious difficulties. As the Court stated in the *Temple of Preah Vihear* case, "the language employed in any given declaration [must] display a clear intention".[25] That is, not any intention, but the intention that the declaration be legally binding on the author State. This does not mean, of course, that, for instance, the United States declaration must contain a provision to the effect that "we consider ourselves legally bound by this declaration"—that would be an anomaly in State practice. A useful reference point is the United States declaration of 6 April 1995 on security assurances to non-nuclear-weapon States, which was criticised by the Group of 21 for its lack of a legally binding character, but which, the United States seemed to believe at the time, was "realistic, serious ... feasible ... [and] credible".[26] The declaration explicitly mentioned "generally recognised principles of international law" before proceeding to state that the United States "reaffirms" its no-first-use of nuclear weapons policy with respect to non-nuclear-weapon States and "affirms its intention" to come to the aid of non-nuclear-weapon States that have come under nuclear attack. Originally issued by the Secretary of State, this declaration was circulated as an official document at the Conference on Disarmament, the United Nations Security Council and the General Assembly, and was mentioned in Security Council Resolution 984.

Even this declaration is not considered to show a clear intention to create legal obligations, however. What then could be said then of President Bush's declaration on TNWs which was not circulated as an official United Nations document, has no reference to international law, and sounds more like a political rather than legal proclamation: "I am therefore directing that the United States eliminate ..." or "we will bring home and destroy ..." or "the United States will withdraw ...".

Analysis of the wording of the United States declaration thus leaves little doubt that it was not meant to create legal obligations. Is their any evidence to the contrary if we look beyond purely a textual interpretation? Subsequent full implementation by the United States of the 1991 TNWs initiatives, particularly in light of the provisions of Article VI of the NPT (which calls on the States to work towards general and complete disarmament), does support the view that the United States may have regarded the declaration not merely as a policy statement, but as a binding commitment. And here is another consideration. On 2 July 1992, President Bush, discussing the status of the earlier TNWs initiatives, pointed out that Russian President Yeltsin "pledged to honour Soviet commitments to take comparable steps reducing tactical nuclear weapons".[27] Evidently, Bush viewed his own statement as a similar commitment, but it is unclear whether a "commitment" in this context implies legal obligations. Lacking clear evidence to support a contrary view, we must conclude that for the United States the TNWs declaration did not create legal consequences. To find otherwise would be to violate a key principle of international law—the notion of State consent.

Although Gorbachev's statement was circulated as an official document in the United Nations Security Council and General Assembly this, of course, is not sufficient to make it binding. Had the Soviet Union asked to register the declaration with the Secretary-General as a legal instrument, as Egypt had done for the Suez declaration, the case for the binding nature of Gorbachev's statement would have been much stronger. The declaration shows little evidence of the Soviet intent to be unilaterally bound. On the contrary, Gorbachev speaks of strict reciprocity with the United States: "the Soviet Union and the United States are taking radical measures on a reciprocal basis ...".[28] At the same time, Gorbachev puts a greater emphasis on the general negotiations then underway: "George Bush's proposals are a fitting continuation of the work begun at Reykjavik"[29] and then again: "by acting in this way—unilaterally, bilaterally and through negotiations, we are decisively advancing the disarmament process".[30] Indeed, it is known that Gorbachev was much more inclined than Bush to proceed with a formal treaty on TNWs. At any rate, reliance on reciprocal measures by the United States suggests that the Soviet declaration cannot be strictly speaking unilateral, being clearly a *quid pro quo* for the earlier United States initiative.

Yeltsin's statement follows up and expands on Gorbachev's declaration. It recognises right away that some steps will be taken "unilaterally", and some "on the basis of reciprocity".[31] Yet later, Yeltsin qualifies his earlier remark: "we are not pursuing unilateral disarmament. The United States is taking parallel steps in a gesture of good will".[32] This qualification, however, falls far short of the strict condition of reciprocity attached to Gorbachev's declaration, which makes it possible to view the declaration as strictly unilateral.

As for its legal effects, the evidence of intent to be bound is not easily discernible in the text of the declaration. Thus, words "we intend to reduce ..." can be viewed as a mere statement of future policy, without reference to legal obligations. Earlier, Yeltsin declares that "Russia confirms its commitment to the policy of radical cuts in nuclear arms", but whether this is a political or a legal commitment is uncertain.[33] Finally, although it is apparent that Russia has to some extent implemented the measures introduced by Gorbachev's and Yeltsin's declarations, there is no publicly available data to indicate to what degree these measures have in fact been enacted. It is therefore unclear whether Russia has indeed complied with its TNWs declarations, as the United States has seemingly done. Thus, Russian intent to be bound by the declarations cannot be inferred from subsequent implementation of the proposed measures.

It is evident from the foregoing, that the three TNWs declarations may not be, in the legal sense, strictly unilateral, certainly not Gorbachev's statement. Even if it is established that they are unilateral, and thus come within the framework of the international law of unilateral acts, difficulties with establishing clear intention to be legally bound suggests that the declarations were statements of policy, which may have created political or moral obligations, but which had no independent legal effects.

A situation may arise when a State is held bound by its own unilateral statement, irrespective of its intent, because of the reliance in good faith on this statement by another State "whereby that other acted to his detriment or the party making the statement has secured some benefit".[34] Such a situation calls into consideration the doctrine of estoppel. In international law, as in municipal law, the basis of estoppel is the "avoidance of inconsistency" in the statements or conduct of States: *allegans contraria non est audiendus*, or, as Lord McNair put it, "you can't blow hot and cold".[35] Thus, as the Finnish reply to the ILC questionnaire on the law of unilateral acts recognised, "a unilateral act is not only binding to the extent that it intends to be so, but also inasmuch as it creates expectations. Thus it may become binding irrespective of the intention of the person making it".[36] Or, as Italy stated in the same questionnaire, "there are unilateral acts that achieve immediate legal effects, and others that create expectations, often irrespective of the real intention of the subject which formulated the act".[37]

For his part, Sir Gerald Fitzmaurice argued that unilateral declarations may create binding obligations "where other countries, on the faith of the Declaration, changed their position or taken action on the basis of it".[38]

The situation of estoppel is not, however, to be presumed; a set of stringent requirements must be satisfied in order for the notion to be properly invoked. For estoppel to hold, there must be a clear representation of fact—"unequivocal in the sense that it can reasonably support the meaning attributed to it by the party raising the plea of estoppel".[39] The classical authority for this is the *Serbian Loans* case, where the PCIJ ruled against the contention that the French bondholders were required to accept payments in French francs, contrary to the terms of the treaty, because they have done so in the past. The Court stated:

> When the requirements of the principle of estoppel to establish a loss of right are considered, it is quite clear that no sufficient basis has been shown for applying the principle in this case. There has been no clear and unequivocal representation of the bondholders upon which the debtor state was entitled to rely and has relied.[40]

In the *Eastern Greenland* case the PCIJ again failed to find evidence of clear representation of fact. In refuting Denmark's contention that Mr. Ihlen's promise to the effect that Norway "would not make any difficulties" for Denmark's claims in Greenland estopped Norway from later adopting a different position, the Court said:

> A careful examination of the words used and of the circumstances in which they were used, as well as of the subsequent developments, shows that M. Ihlen cannot have meant to be giving there a definite recognition of Danish sovereignty over Greenland, and shows also that he cannot have been understood by the Danish Government at the time as having done so.[41]

The ICJ has been just as reluctant to admit the existence of estoppel. In the *North Sea Continental Shelf* case, the Court rejected arguments by Denmark and Netherlands to the effect that Germany was estopped from denying the applicability of the 1958 Geneva Convention on the Continental Shelf by reason of its past conduct. The Court found that there must be a "very definite, very consistent course of conduct" for this to be the case.[42]

Evidently, representation of fact must not only be clear and unequivocal, but also unconditional, in the sense that it cannot be made "in the course of negotiations with a view to a settlement which does not materialise, or ... subject to conditions later unfulfilled by the other party".[43] As the Court stated in the *Advisory Opinion on the European Commission of the Danube* case:

> ... though it is perfectly true that the three delegates of France, Great Britain and Italy ... declared that they would agree to leave to the Roumanian authorities the enforcement of the regulations ... it is equally true that this proposal was made dependent upon conditions which were not accepted by the Roumanian government. No agreement was therefore reached...[44]

One instance where the Court did find a clear representation of fact was the case concerning *the Arbitral Award made by the King of Spain on 23 December 1906*. The Court, not convinced by Nicaragua's contention that the arbitral award in an earlier dispute to which it was a party was invalid, ruled that:

> In the judgement of the Court, Nicaragua, by express declaration and by conduct, recognised the Award as valid and it is no longer open to Nicaragua to go back upon that recognition and to challenge the validity of the Award. Nicaragua's failure to raise any question with regard to the validity of the Award for several years ... further confirms the conclusion at which the Court has arrived.[45]

Here, however, as Sir Ian Sinclair pointed out, the Court carefully avoided making an explicit reference to estoppel, because another condition was left unsatisfied—the reliance in good faith by the other party on Nicaragua's conduct to the detriment of that party or to Nicaragua's benefit.

International tribunals have generally been reluctant to find the condition of reliance in good faith satisfied. An interesting exception is the *Temple of Preah Vihear* case, in which Thailand rejected the validity of a map, drawn in connection with the 1904 boundary treaty between Siam and France, the latter acting as the protecting power of Cambodia. The Court ruled:

> Even if there were any doubt as to Siam's acceptance of the map in 1908, and hence of the frontier indicated thereon, the Court would consider, in the light of the subsequent course of events, that Thailand is now precluded by her conduct from asserting that she did not accept it. She has, for fifty years, enjoyed such benefits as the treaty of 1904 conferred on her, if only the benefit of a stable frontier.[46]

However, in the *North Sea Continental* Case, cited above, the ICJ ruled that Germany's conduct, apart from evidencing the acceptance of the 1958 regime, also had not caused "Denmark or the Netherlands, in reliance on such conduct, detrimentally to change their position or suffer some prejudice. Of this there is no evidence whatever in the present case".[47] In the *Tinoco* arbitration, Judge Taft, refusing to accept Costa Rica's view that non-recognition by the United Kingdom of the Tinoco government precluded it from asserting rights conferred by that government, ruled as follows:

> The failure to recognise the de facto government did not lead the succeeding government to change its position in any way on the faith of it. ... a person claiming the estoppel [must have been led] into a position in which the truth will injury him. There is no such a case here.[48]

Coming back to the TNWs declarations, the wording of all three statements is clear and unequivocal, so that there is little doubt about what it is that Bush, Gorbachev and later Yeltsin have promised to do, and both the United States and Russia are entitled to rely on these promises in good faith, for here we have an unambiguous representation of fact. As stated above, representation of fact must be unconditional. Bush's statement refers to the expectation of comparable Soviet response, but it is not conditioned on reciprocity. If the Soviets fail to match the actions of the United States, the statement goes on to say, "a historic opportunity will have been lost", but certainly this will not undo the American initiative.[49] Gorbachev's statement, however, explicitly refers to a *quid pro quo*—"proposals we are making in response" and "measures on a reciprocal basis"; this is clearly a conditional declaration, and as such, it cannot serve as the basis for estoppel.[50] Yeltsin, interestingly, unconditionally reaffirms and expands on the Soviet commitments, but attaches conditions to further proposed cuts. In his statement, only unconditional commitments may give rise to estoppel, if third parties relied in good faith on these commitments and thereby suffered or benefited Russia.

In this connection, a problematic distinction must be addressed. Dr. Bowett, in his landmark article on "Estoppel Before International Tribunals and its Relation to Acquiescence", noted that:

> ... the representation involved in a course of conduct must, apparently, be made to or directed to the party which pleads the estoppel: a party cannot rely upon statements which are not addressed to it and which are not intended to or likely to affect its course of action.[51]

The apparent authority for this is the *Croft* case, in which it was held that the United Kingdom could not rely on one Portuguese decree, submitted to Portugal's Council of Senate.[52] It is reasonable, of course, to apply this restriction "in a purely *inter partes* issue", but, as Judge Weeramantry suggested in his Separate Opinion in the *Gabcikovo* case, "we have entered an era of international law in which international law subserves not only the interests of individual States, but looks beyond them and their parochial concerns to the greater interests of humanity and planetary welfare".[53]

Thus, the conduct or declarations of a State in an *inter partes* issue with global implications may allow third parties to plead estoppel, inasmuch as a representation of fact in such an issue, even if it was not addressed to third parties or was intended for the domestic audience, is a representation *erga omnes*. Needless to say, this applies to TNWs, just as it does to all weapons of mass destruction.

In order for the plea of estoppel to be properly invoked, it must be shown that States, in relying in good faith on the TNWs declarations of either the United States or Russia, suffered detriment or benefited the declarant States. Now, the United States declaration and subsequent elimination and removal of TNWs, as pledged, provide a clear representation of fact. It is evident, moreover, that both the Soviet Union and Russia have relied on the United States declaration and have taken steps to remove to central storage and eliminate some—we do not know how many—tactical nuclear weapons. In fact, Yeltsin's declaration is absolutely explicit about the raison d'être of Russia's actions: "I want to emphasize that we are not pursuing unilateral disarmament. The United States is taking parallel steps in a gesture of good will".[54] By implication, Russia relied in good faith on the United States to keep to its pledge, and even recognised, that Washington, too, could rely in good faith on

Moscow's promises. If at this stage, for example, the United States decided to reintroduce nuclear warheads to Tomahawk Cruise Missiles, the plea of estoppel by Russia would stand a good chance, inasmuch as Russia, in relying on the United States to remove nuclear warheads from surface ships, did the same and incurred costs or suffered some prejudice. It is always difficult, of course, to show that the State pleading estoppel has in fact suffered detriment, this is one of the reasons why the international tribunals have rarely upheld pleas of estoppel. Should Poland, for example, claim that Russia is now estopped from moving tactical nukes to its naval basis in Kaliningrad Oblast (representation of fact here is clear, noting the 1991/92 declarations and even earlier pledges by Gorbachev to keep the Baltics nuclear-free, and Russia has repeatedly made assurances at the highest level that it does not have TNWs in Kaliningrad) Poland would have to show how it suffered detriment from its reliance on the Russian conduct—it is not immediately apparent that it did. In other words, viewing the TNWs statements as unilateral declarations giving rise to estoppel is not an altogether hopeless enterprise under international law, but one must keep in mind that the existence of estoppel is not easily proved, even when all requirements have been satisfied. This is only natural considering the seriousness of the notion of estoppel—that is, binding a State to a certain course of conduct irrespective of its intent.

I began this paper by asking the question of whether the 1991/92 declarations on TNWs by the United States and the Soviet Union/Russia could have binding effects on these States under international law—that is, whether they could give rise to legal obligations to reduce or eliminate parts of their respective TNWs arsenals. The answer is... may be. There are good arguments for regarding these declarations as a form of international agreement, falling under the framework of treaty law, but the notion of State consent looms large in the background: a State cannot be said to have entered into a treaty unless it intended to do so.

States may bind themselves by unilateral declarations they make, if they clearly so intend. There is simply not enough evidence that the United States, the USSR and Russia intended to undertake binding commitments on the TNWs.

Irrespective of whether the TNW declarations were strictly speaking unilateral and whether the declarant States intended for them to be legally binding, however, these declarations evidence clear representation of fact and, as such, may justify a plea of estoppel, if it demonstrated that other States relied on these declarations to their detriment or to the benefit of the declarant States. As this paper indicates, the possibility of estoppel is not precluded in the present case. Yet estoppel is an often-invoked principle, which the international tribunals are reluctant to uphold.

Black and white are rare colours in international law, particularly in the shady area of nuclear weapons, where politics and law are closely intertwined. The best case, then, that can be made for the TNW declarations is that there is a possibility that they may give rise to binding obligations. How likely a possibility this is, is difficult to say, but likely enough to warrant a close consideration of legal issues involved.

Endnotes

1. A/CN.4/519, p. 28, paragraph 123.
2. Ibid., p. 29.
3. Ibid., p. 34.
4. Ibid., p. 33.
5. PCIJ Reports, Series A, No. 10, 1927, p. 18.
6. Sir Gerald Fitzmaurice, "The Law and Procedure of the International Court of Justice 1950-54. Treaty Interpretation and Other Treaty Points", *British Yearbook of International Law*, Vol. 33, 1957, p. 230.
7. Ibid., p. 231.
8. Ibid.
9. "Address to the Nation on Reducing United States and Soviet Nuclear Weapons", (Bush's statement), 27 September 1991, http://bushlibrary.tamu.edu/papers/1991/91092704.html, p. 2.
10. Ibid., p. 4.
11. A/46/592 (Gorbachev's statement), 5 October 1991, p. 2.
12. ICJ, 1952, p. 103.
13. "Address to the Nation on Reducing United States and Soviet Nuclear Weapons", p. 2.
14. Fitzmaurice, p. 230.
15. A/CN.4/511, p. 17.
16. ICJ Report, 1962, pp. 417-418.
17. M. Whiteman, *Digest of International Law*, Vol. 3, 1964, p. 1126.
18. A/CN.4/511, p. 14.
19. Ibid., p. 15.
20. Ibid., p. 16.

21. Ibid.
22. ICJ Reports, 1986, p. 132, paragraph 261.
23. Ibid., p. 573, paragraph 39.
24. ICJ Reports, 1974, p. 267, paragraph 43.
25. ICJ Reports, 1961, p. 32.
26. S/PV.3514, 11 April 1995, p. 26.
27. "Statement on the United States Nuclear Weapons Initiative", 2 July 1992, http://bushlibrary.tamu.edu/papers/1992/92070202.htmi.
28. A/46/592 (Gorbachev's statement), p. 2.
29. Ibid.
30. Ibid., p. 4.
31. "On Russia's Policy in the Field of Arms Limitation and Reduction" (Yeltsin's Statement), 29 January 1992, http://www.unog.ch/unidir/tnwrfstmt.htm.
32. Ibid.
33. Ibid.
34. D.W. Bowett, "Estoppel Before International Tribunals and its Relation to Acquiescence", *British Yearbook of International Law*, Vol. 33, 1957, p. 201.
35. McNair (Lord), *The Law of Treaties*, Oxford: Clarendon Press, 1961, p. 485.
36. A/CN.4/511, p. 15.
37. Ibid.
38. Fitzmaurice, p. 230.
39. Bowett, p. 184.
40. PCIJ Reports, Series A, No. 20, 1929, p. 5.
41. PCIJ Reports, Series A/B, No. 53, 1933, p. 69.
42. ICJ Reports, 1969, p. 26, paragraph 28.
43. Bowett, p. 191.
44. PCIJ Reports, Series B, No. 14, 1927, p. 6.
45. ICJ Reports, 1960, pp. 213-214.
46. ICJ Reports, 1962, p. 32.
47. ICJ Reports, 1969, p. 26.
48. *American Journal of International Law*, Vol. 18, 1924, p. 156.
49. Bush's statement, p. 4.
50. Gorbachev's statement, p. 2.
51. Bowett, p. 186.
52. Moore's International Arbitrations, Vol. V, 1898, pp. 4979-83.
53. ICJ Reports, 1997, p. 118.
54. Yeltsin's statement.

CHAPTER 10

STRENGTHENING THE 1991 DECLARATIONS: VERIFICATION AND TRANSPARENCY COMPONENTS

Nikolai Sokov

Ten years after the 1991 unilateral, parallel declarations of George Bush and Mikhail Gorbachev on tactical nuclear weapons (TNWs), the future of the regime they created is more precarious than ever. On the one hand, these declarations have resulted in the elimination and deactivation of thousands of nuclear warheads, and thus have succeeded better than any formal treaty. TNWs are no longer deployed on land and sea, while the number of air-launched short-range nuclear weapons has declined dramatically. Understandable enthusiasm about this method of nuclear arms reductions, however, is tempered by the steady increase of interest in military applications of tactical nuclear weapons while the regime itself remains informal and easy to withdraw from.

Inclusion of language pertaining to the reduction of TNWs in the Final Document of the 2000 Non-Proliferation Treaty (NPT) Review Conference was just about the only positive development in the last several years. Unfortunately, chances that it will be acted upon by the United States and Russia appear slim.

In both the United States and Russia arguments have surfaced in favour of the utility of TNWs and even of the development of a new generation of such weapons. Although the missions for TNWs proposed in Russia and the United States differ, all proposals include the use of tactical nuclear weapons in actual warfighting—whether vis-à-vis qualitatively and/or quantitatively superior conventional forces or for strikes against hardened targets in "rogue States. " Nuclear laboratories in both countries advocate the development of new types of nuclear warheads for these "limited" missions—low-yield, highly accurate, capable of destroying hardened underground facilities.

Following the 11 September terrorist attacks, there have been calls in the United States for the use of TNWs in anti-terrorist operations. Although there is no reason to believe that these calls will be heeded, they have served to bolster interest in the potential utility of TNWs. Under these conditions the "calculated ambiguity" with regard to the possible use of nuclear weapons can be harmful for the future of the nuclear non-proliferation regime if only because it casts doubt on the continued adherence of the United States to the negative security guarantees, which were adopted by all nuclear-weapon States in conjunction with the NPT.

The uncertain future of the 1991/92 TNWs regime should be a cause of concern. It would create the perception that nuclear-weapon States have abandoned their obligation to seek the complete elimination of nuclear weapons and consequently might negatively affect the status of Article VI of the NPT. The perceived utility of TNWs, promoted by various, often authoritative, figures in the United States and Russia, might inadvertently increase the inclination of a number of States to seek to acquire nuclear weapons because of their expected tangible contribution to security. Practical steps toward the development of new types of TNWs will spell trouble for the Comprehensive Test Ban Treaty (CTBT) since the development of such weapons will almost certainly involve testing. Thus, the importance of the 1991/92 informal TNWs regime extends clearly beyond the weapons themselves.

CHALLENGES TO THE INFORMAL TNWs REGIME

Just as the end of the Cold War has "rearranged" perceptions of security threats, the current challenges to arms control regimes no longer stem from the threat of an arms race. In fact, both the United States and Russia are planning to reduce their nuclear arsenals, and even the possible modernisation of TNWs will hardly reverse this trend. Rather, the greatest threat to the 1991/92 regime stems from indifference in the United States and Russia to arms control regimes in general and the increasingly visible preference for unilateralism in decisions with regard to the optimisation and reduction of nuclear arsenals.

Each side has relatively few concerns about the tactical nuclear arsenal of the other and, more importantly, these concerns are apparently not sufficiently acute to instigate concessions to the other side to address them. For example, the United States has expressed concern about the lack of information with regard to TNWs in Russia, while Russia has expressed concern about United States tactical nuclear weapons in Europe. Neither seems interested in strengthening the existing regime in ways that would address these and other issues, however. Each seems to prefer to retain a relative freedom of action, even if that entails freedom of action for the other.

As the relationship between the United States and Russia has improved and the perceived threat emanating from the other's nuclear weapons has decreased, the perceived need for nuclear arms control measures has plummeted as well. Both sides, no longer locked in confrontation, now tend to pay more attention to what in the short-run may represent the negative side of treaties, such as the high cost of reductions and verification, constraints on cost-effective optimisation, etc.

This phenomenon is particularly evident in the area of strategic nuclear weapons. The United States seems rather unconcerned about what Russia might do in the absence of arms control treaties, while Russia is concerned primarily not with the level of the United States nuclear arsenal *per se*, but rather with the possibility that this might increase sharply and unpredictably. The same attitudes may hold even more strongly with regards to TNWs.

For example, in the context of the optimal structuring of its nuclear arsenal (with specific threats in mind such as broadly defined threats emanating "from the South"), Russia might decide to re-deploy nuclear warheads on land-based short-range missiles even as its overall TNWs arsenal continues to shrink. The United States, for similar reasons, might decide to deploy tactical nuclear weapons outside its territory—in the Persian Gulf or East Asia—in the context of the continuing counter-terrorist operation. Under present conditions these or other steps will not immediately generate suspicion and fear on the other side, but the 1991/92 declarations will collapse. Then TNWs would once again become a class of weapons completely unregulated by international regimes.

Another reason for the 1991/92 regime's vulnerability is its rigidity, which, counterintuitively, stems from its informal nature. Although theoretically the United States and Russia could create a new informal regime, the probability of this appears low: the fall of 1991, when American and Soviet leaders made their unilateral, parallel statements, was a relatively rare time when the objectives and interests of the two countries with regard to TNWs coincided almost perfectly. It is difficult to imagine that the two countries could easily agree on a new set of limitations on their freedom of action: at least, their current policies do not suggest that such an option is feasible. If, of the other hand, they simply agree, whether expressly or by default, to allow the other side complete freedom of action, such an arrangement could hardly qualify as an international regime since it would lack the central characteristic of any international regime—the provision of predictability.

The deterioration of the 1991/92 regime, in spite of its many drawbacks, would be a serious loss for international security. The main function of any international regime is to provide predictability about the capabilities and intentions of participants through the exchange of information or verifiable prohibitions on certain courses of action. Predictability reduces the propensity for planning based on worst-case scenarios. The collapse of the TNWs regime is likely to remove whatever limited degree of predictability exists today with respect to these weapons, and one cannot rule out gradual increases of suspicions. The debate over the missile defence system which the United States plans to deploy and the fate of the Anti-Ballistic Missile (ABM) Treaty demonstrate how quickly actions that are ostensibly not directed at the other party can have a ripple effect on the relationship as a whole. Reports about the deployment of Russian TNWs in the Kaliningrad Oblast, which emerged in January 2001 and have never been fully substantiated, illustrate how quickly suspicions can emerge and how unsettling they can be.

Intentions do not necessarily matter in inter-State relations. States tend to equate the capabilities of other States with likely actions; that is, if the one State has the capability to act, other States prepare to balance that capability "just in case", paying little heed to statements about the absence of dangerous intentions. The risk that unused capabilities can translate into policy is a foundation for all or almost all existing arms control agreements: they remove capabilities for waging war or using certain types of weapons rather than the intentions to take these actions.

Unfortunately, the negative consequences of the demise of international regimes can often be fully appreciated only much later as suspicions and insecurity begin to mount in the absence of adequate mechanisms to remove or alleviate these concerns. If the demise of the TNWs regime happens with the tacit or even explicit agreement of both sides, at first it will hardly generate a major crisis. A crisis is likely to occur, but considerably later.

One can agree that the bilateral arms control agreements characteristic of the Cold War era might no longer be necessary, especially if the United States and Russia continue to build down their arsenals, but it seems inadvisable to simply discard them. Prudence dictates that they should be replaced with new regimes. In fact, even today, as the United States prepares to formally withdraw from the ABM Treaty, consultations on a new framework and possibly a new legally binding agreement are underway. Compared to the TNWs regime, the ABM Treaty demonstrated greater resilience of legally binding regimes. The United States took years to make the decision to withdraw, the consequences of such a step became clearer as a result of an extensive debate both inside the United States and in the international community in general, and the very presence of the ABM Treaty facilitated the decision to discuss a replacement regime. Unfortunately similar discussions are not conducted with regard to TNWs, and the probability that the United States and Russia will address this issue is extremely low.

TRANSPARENCY AND VERIFICATION—THE WAY TO SAVE THE TNWs REGIME

We seem to have arrived at a junction where we face a choice between the inevitable collapse of the TNWs regime at some point in the not-so-distant future and taking steps to salvage it. To avoid an increase of distrust and planning based on worst-case scenarios it is necessary to seriously think about ways of preserving the gist of the 1991/92 regime, possibly by giving it a new form. In the present world, in the light of improved bilateral relations, the United States and Russia, indeed, probably do not need limits on the types and classes of weapons they are allowed to deploy. The element, which is truly needed, however, is reliable knowledge of the other side's arsenal, its status, and its capabilities so that "unpleasant surprises" and suspicions are ruled out. In other words, both the United States and Russia can benefit from the ability to prevent or quickly clarify situations such as the one that emerged over the suspected deployment of TNWs in the Kaliningrad Oblast.

The central drawback of the 1991/92 regime, however, is precisely the absence of transparency and verification provisions, that is, of reliable information about the numbers, locations, and types of tactical nuclear weapons, as well as of timely, preferably advance, knowledge about any changes in the posture of TNWs. Without doubt, verification is the most challenging aspect of tactical nuclear weapons and also one of the key reasons why in 1991 the two countries decided to stop at unilateral, parallel declarations instead of negotiating a formal, verifiable agreement. Still, there seems to be no other choice but to try to develop this particular area, whether in addition to or in-place of existing limitations on the deployable categories of weapons.

Existing arms control agreements between Russia and the United States provide predictability primarily through substantive limitations (ceilings on the number of warheads, limits on modernisation, etc.) while verification serves as an important supporting tool that helps ensure compliance. Under the present circumstances, however, both sides apparently are no longer interested in the same level of detailed and exhaustive substantive limitations simply because they are less concerned about each other's actions and are interested in imposing constraints only on very limited, isolated courses of action. Instead, transparency should to assume a more prominent place on the arms control agenda. It can help to ensure predictability and avoid mutual suspicions even in the absence of substantive limitations. If the limitations on deployment patterns, established by the 1991/92 declarations, crumble without substitution, availability of reliable information on the status of arsenals can at least prevent a bilateral crisis between the United States and Russia and lay the foundation for subsequent reductions.

For these reasons, it seems advisable to concentrate on developing a system of measures that ensure verifiable transparency. Some substantive limitations might be needed as well—for example, Russia seems unwilling to address TNWs transparency without also addressing the stationing of American TNWs in Europe—but the number and the scope of such provisions can remain limited.

A verification system for a TNWs regime should, understandably, address warheads rather than delivery vehicles (as was the case in previous nuclear arms control agreements). All or nearly all TNWs delivery systems for are dual-use, or, if they require modifications to carry nuclear warheads, the attending differences are difficult to verify. Consequently, one cannot apply the Strategic Arms Reductions Treaty (START) accounting rules, which assume that every delivery vehicle is equipped with nuclear warheads.

To be effective as a means of conveying predictability, measures that ensure transparency and verification should perform the following functions:

- provide information on the status of TNWs arsenals;
- provide information about changes in the location of warheads; and
- warn about increases in the alert status of tactical nuclear forces.

The last goal appears particularly important in the light of the negative Russian reaction to the proposal on the exchange of data, which the United States put forth in January 2000. According to that proposal, data exchange was supposed to cover all strategic and non-strategic nuclear warheads, as well as components and fissile materials obtained during their disassembly, and a number of other categories. Russia's negative reaction derived at least in part from its dissatisfaction with the lack of provisions on, for example, advance warning about the change in status (preparation for forward deployment or use) of United States TNWs deployed in Europe, including the possibility of their deployment on the territories of new North Atlantic Treaty Organisation (NATO) members.

In other words, data exchange in and of itself does not necessarily lead to an increase in security. As such it should be coupled with measures that ensure advance warning about steps that might be interpreted as preparations for use or threat of use of these weapons. Without such warning, transparency will have very limited utility, or, at worse, proposals on data exchange will be simply rejected (as happened in 2000).

In the light of concerns about the costs and inconveniences of verification, these measures should also entail as few disruptions in the normal operation of facilities, personnel and weapons as possible. The current status of the United States-Russian relationship probably allows for the relaxation of the rigid and highly demanding procedures that are characteristic of the Intermediate Nuclear Forces (INF) and START Treaties.

It seems advisable to build the verification regime in a modular fashion, that is, to create a set of "building blocks" that could be introduced sequentially depending on what the sides need or are prepared to accept at a particular moment in time. For example, there are some basic measures that could be implemented right away but that can be expanded at a later date if the decision is made to conclude a formal treaty. Similarly, one set of measures is needed to verify the status of deployed weapons, whereas verification of their dismantlement would require a more complex and intrusive set of provisions. The modular approach should allow the transparency system to expand without renegotiating everything from scratch.

The measures proposed below are intended to cover only warheads for tactical (short-range) delivery systems. One should be mindful, however, of the potential "verification gap" that could develop if warheads for strategic delivery vehicles are left outside the regime. For example, one side might question whether the unannounced transit of nuclear warheads involved strategic or tactical weapons. Thus, the proposed verification regime would be most effective if it encompassed all categories of warheads. An added benefit of including strategic nuclear warheads into the proposed regime is the ability to drop many of the limitations and verification provisions of START I, thereby reducing its cost of operation. Furthermore, a transparency regime that covers strategic warheads as well, can help resolve the differences between Russia and the United States with regard to the latter's plan of reducing of its nuclear arsenal through downloading (i.e., removing and storing warheads) by addressing the possibility of clandestine uploading the return of warheads to delivery vehicles.

The transparency regime could consist of the following levels:

I. Alert status of warheads for tactical delivery systems

1. Information exchange at this level may be elementary and include only the overall numbers (possibly also by category, i.e., intended for air-, sea- or land-based delivery vehicles) and their locations. Provision of numbers is a basic confidence-building measure,

which should not necessarily be verifiable at this juncture. Exchange of information about locations is the key element that is intended create conditions for advance warning about changes in the alert status of warheads, including their movement to forward areas or to bases where delivery vehicles are deployed.

2. Assurances that warheads do not leave their storage facilities can entail "corralling" them within designated facilities approximately following the rules of the Perimeter and Portal Continuous Monitoring (PPCM) system established by the INF and START I Treaties. One important exception can be the use of distance monitoring of the perimeter and the portal to avoid the permanent presence of monitors at each facility. Remote sensors should allow detection of the movement of warheads through the portal. When warheads are removed from these secured facilities, movement should involve small numbers and be subject to advance notification. Such notifications can include the date of movement, its purpose (i.e., taking them to another storage facility, to a dismantlement facility, or for reassembly/maintenance)—more or less following notifications about items in transit provided under START I.

3. It may be advisable to agree upon baseline inspections of former warhead storage sites to ensure that no warheads are kept there at the moment of the regime's entry into force. Similarly, it is advisable to conduct closeout inspections of storage facilities after all warheads are permanently removed from them.

4. This set of measures can (probably even should) include the right of suspect-site inspections to ensure that there are no undeclared places where unaccounted warheads are kept. Such inspections should be rare, however, since warhead storage sites have unique signatures.

This level of transparency can guarantee that warheads kept at military bases are not mated with delivery vehicles without warning and that warheads kept at central storage facilities are not moved secretly to military bases where they could be mated with delivery vehicles. Forward deployment might be suspected, for example, if a significant number of warheads are relocated to storage sites in the same area.

An important precondition for the introduction of this stage of a transparency regime is that nuclear weapons are not deployed on ships and submarines, although the transfer of warheads to naval bases would become possible and subject to verification if a decision to change the deployment pattern envisioned in the 1991/92 declaration is made.

These measures should encompass storage facilities outside national territories (currently, only the American TNWs in Europe, but if there were additional deployments outside either American or Russian national territory, these too would be included).

The measures would be able to survive a decision by either side to amend the deployment pattern proscribed by the 1991/92 declarations, such as the deployment of nuclear warheads on land-based missiles or the stationing of warheads beyond national frontiers. Thus, they would increase the flexibility of both sides and would help alleviate the possible negative consequences of amending the commitments contained in the declarations with sustained transparency.

II. Verification of the elimination of warheads

These measures can be used either in conjunction with any other levels of verification or separately—as part of the on-going effort to secure fissile materials obtained from dismantled warheads (under certain conditions dismantlement of weapons might require verification that particular shipments of fissile materials originated from warheads). The relevant regime can include, but not be limited to, the following:

1. Each side would designate the dismantlement facility—either separately or as part of a larger existing facility (in that case it would be necessary to differentiate between the dismantlement and maintenance/reassembly parts).

2. The warhead designated for dismantlement would be taken into the disassembly room; the room would be checked by inspectors in advance and all exits would be sealed; disassembly would be conducted without inspectors present, but these would be able to observe all exits that were not sealed.

3. After disassembly was completed, inspectors would be allowed back into the room where they could observe the fissile materials removed from the warhead (possibly placed in a proper container), the outer shell of the warhead (or, using INF Treaty terms, "front section, minus nuclear warhead device and guidance elements"), and possibly some other elements as agreed upon.

4. Fissile materials would then be shipped to the storage facility with appropriate notifications and a check-in procedure at the destination. The rest of the warhead could be disposed of following agreed procedures; for example, it seems advisable to eliminate the outer shell of the warhead according to the procedures specified in the INF Treaty.

5. Remanufacturing facilities (or sections of facilities designated for remanufacturing) might be equipped with a PPCM system similar to the one around storage facilities to demonstrate that the number of warheads taken inside for remanufacturing equals the number of warheads leaving the facility (so that secret manufacturing is impossible). This measure does not appear absolutely necessary, however, because the overall number of warheads in possession of each side can be verified indirectly by keeping track of the number of warheads sent from storage facilities for remanufacturing and the number of warheads returned to storage.

Taken in conjunction with notifications about the movement of warheads to dismantlement facilities, these measures can guarantee that warheads are not taken to a secret location under the pretext of dismantlement. The scheme outlined above follows the warhead dismantlement verification procedures developed by the Russian nuclear laboratory in Snezhinsk under contract with the United States Department of Energy.

III. Limit on the overall number of warheads

The following steps can be agreed to in addition to the measures described above:

1. The sides agree to exchange information about the number of warheads at each location.

2. They also agree to baseline data inspections involving one visit to each storage facility to verify the declared number of warheads. After that, the same "corralling" and notification regime will apply as above, and there will be no need for inspectors to revisit the facilities.

This stage should probably be part of a rather robust, legally binding agreement and, in any event, should likely correspond to the stage when the two sides decide to limit the number of their tactical nuclear warheads to more or less equal levels.

These measures can also be used—maybe on a more limited scale, involving verification of numbers only at select facilities—if the two sides decide to establish area or category limits. For example, a limit on the number of warheads kept within a certain region (limits on concentration of weapons, similar to the approach utilised in the Conventional Forces in Europe (CFE) Treaty) or a limit on the number of warheads kept at naval bases, etc.

Finally, verifiable exchanges of data on the number of warheads kept at individual facilities can help to enforce a limit on the number of deployed weapons (i.e., warheads kept at military bases readily available for mating with delivery vehicles). This measure might be particularly useful, possibly even indispensable, with regard to warheads for strategic delivery vehicles since the United States has decided to retain a significant uploading capability.

The approaches outlined above could also be applied to other countries that might join a TNWs or a broader nuclear arms control regime in the future.

CONCLUSION

We are now in a period when nuclear arms control is simply no longer fashionable, especially among the nuclear-weapon States. The immediate danger, which emanated from the global confrontation and the risk of nuclear war, has disappeared or at least receded. Treaties are no longer viewed as vital to security; instead, the costs of treaty implementation attract more attention than ever and generate a desire to withdraw from, or at least limit the intrusiveness of relevant procedures. Both the United States and Russia plan deeper reductions of their nuclear arsenals than any existing treaty mandates. Optimisation of arsenals for survivability, cost-effectiveness, modernisation and replacement or other reasons also encourages withdrawal from agreements. Each nuclear-weapon State is less concerned about how the others might respond to its nuclear arsenal. Against this backdrop, one finds it difficult to argue for not only saving, but, instead, enhancing the rather weak, informal TNWs arms control regime.

This task is both vital and urgent, however. It might be useful to think about salvaging the TNWs regime as a means of laying the groundwork for salvaging and maybe recasting the whole system of arms control regimes that we know today. Introducing verifiable transparency measures for the TNWs regime might help in the development of a broader, more comprehensive arms control regime for all types and classes of nuclear weapons, relegating to the past the existing treaties, which are sometimes cumbersome and expensive to implement. Of course, it goes without saying that even old and imperfect instruments should not be discarded until something new is available to replace them. This is why the title of this chapter refers to the "strengthening" rather than the "replacement" of the 1991/92 declarations.

CHAPTER 11

THE SEPTEMBER 1991 PRESIDENTIAL NUCLEAR INITIATIVES AND THE ELIMINATION, STORING AND SECURITY ASPECTS OF TNWS

Joshua Handler*

OVERVIEW

The unilateral declarations exchanged by the Presidents of the United States and the Soviet Union in 1991 concerning tactical nuclear weapons (TNWs) were neither treaties nor empty promises. They were public pledges to take specific disarmament steps, for the most part unconditionally. The key commitments comprised in the declarations were to remove, eliminate and consolidate, either in part or in their entirety, certain categories of TNWs.[1] This chapter reviews the status of implementation of the declarations and offers an assessment—from a non-governmental organisation (NGO) perspective—about the current status of TNWs, their safety compared to other nuclear weapons and their future.

Table 1 summarises the commitments made by Presidents Bush, Gorbachev and Yeltsin in September 1991, October 1991, January 1992 and President Clinton's September 1994 Nuclear Posture Review (NPR) in regards to the removal, elimination and consolidation of TNWs. President Clinton's NPR is included as it had some important implications for the American TNWs force and can be seen as a follow-on to the steps taken by the other presidents in 1991-1992.

Table 2 summarises the details of the American TNWs to be removed, eliminated and consolidated under the presidential declarations.[2]

The figures of United States TNWs provided are noteworthy because they are the first such figures released by the United States. 1,700 of 2,150

Lance and artillery warheads were deployed overseas and 450 were kept in the United States. Importantly, at least 3,050 warheads in total were to be eliminated—850 Lance, 1,300 artillery and 900 B-57 depth bombs. Note, due to the controversy over deployment of enhanced radiation (ER) or "neutron bombs" in Europe in the late-1970s and 1980s, the ER warhead versions of Lance missiles and the W-79 8in artillery shell were not deployed overseas but kept in the United States.

Table 1

	Presidents Bush and ***Clinton***[3]	Presidents Gorbachev and ***Yeltsin***[4]
Army	- **Eliminate All**—missiles, artillery - Proposed to eliminate mines (US no longer deployed)	- **Eliminate All**—missiles, artillery, "mines" - **Confirm**
Navy	- **Remove All**—from ships, submarines and land-based aircraft - Eliminate "many"—**Store rest centrally** - Propose USSR to do likewise - **Denuclearises surface fleet** - **Keep sea-launched cruise missiles (SLCMs)**	- **Remove All**—from ships, submarines and land-based aircraft - Eliminate Some—**Store rest in central bases** - **Proposed to eliminate all if US agreed** - **Eliminate 1/3**
Air Force	- **Remove from Korea** - Eliminate "many"—**Store rest centrally** - Propose USSR to do likewise - Keep weapons in Europe - **Keep weapons in Europe and US Dual-Capable Aircraft (DCA)**	- Proposed to transfer to central storage sites if the US agreed to do the same - **Eliminate 1/2** - **Repeats transfer proposal**
Air Defence	- Proposed to USSR to eliminate all (US no longer deployed)	- **Remove All**—from operational forces - Eliminate Some—**Store rest in central bases** - **Eliminate 1/2**

Table 2

Army (and Marine Corps)
Eliminate all ~2,150 missile and artillery weapons Lance missile—eliminate 850 Lance warheads (~150 ER in US) Artillery—eliminate ~1,300 artillery shells 3 types—two 8 in and one 155 mm W-33 8 in ~500 to be returned to US W-48 155mm ~ 500 W-48s to be returned to US W-79 8 in—(W79-1 ER in US)—all to be eliminated
Navy
Remove ~500 TNWs from sea surface ships and submarines B-57 Depth Bomb—Eliminate all ~900 land- and sea-deployed SLCMs ~100 returned to the US
Air Force (Navy/Marine Corps*) Strike Bombs
B-57 Strike bomb*—Keep, but some eliminated Tactical bomb—**B61-2* -5***/B61-3,-4,-10—Keep B-61

President Clinton's 1994 NPR, moreover, denuclearized United States surface ships. This meant that nuclear SLCM capability was removed. In addition, United States aircraft carriers no longer carried B61 bombs for strike aircraft, and as a result the -2 and -5 mods were dismantled.

The United States had deployed many other types of TNWs, but these—such as Army Atomic Demolition Munitions (ADM), Ground-launched Cruise Missile (GLCM), Honest John and Pershing 1a and 2 missiles and Navy missiles, ASROC and SUBROC ASW rockets—were retired prior to the 1991-92 declaration and hence not included in the latter. Their warheads were dismantled during the 1980s and 1990s, except for the GLCM W84 warhead, which is retained in the inactive stockpile.[5]

In terms of removing TNWs from deployment, the United States implemented its commitments under its declarations relatively quickly. Table 3 summarises the years by which this was accomplished for Army, Navy and Air Force TNWs and by place of deployment.

Table 3

	Accomplished by			
	1991	**1992**	**1993**	**1994**
Army				
Europe		Y[6]		
Republic of Korea	Y[7]			
US				Y[8]
Navy				
Surface Ships		Y		
Submarines		Y		
Aircraft		Y		
Air Force				
Europe			Y[9]	
Republic of Korea	Y			

Table 4 summarises the current status of the United States' programme of elimination of TNWs. The United States did not promise initially to finish implementing the declarations by a particular date. It appears, however, that the United States has been making steady progress in eliminating those weapons it promised to liquidate. An important exception, however, is the W-79 nuclear artillery shell. Elimination only started in 1998 and is scheduled to be completed in 2003.[10] Confusingly, the data provided by the DOE does not entirely match the information given by United States officials in 1991 about the number of TNWs to be eliminated. For example, it appears more Lance missile warheads were eliminated than were stated to exist in 1991. Moreover, there are some gaps in the data such as: the number of W-33 artillery warheads eliminated and the dates of starting and completing elimination; how many W-79 artillery warheads were to be eliminated and what will be total Army warheads eliminated; does the 2,242 B-57 bomb warheads equal all the B-57 depth-bomb and strike variants and; what portion of the 1,159 B-61 bomb warheads dismantled are B61-2 and -5 mods.

Table 4

Warhead	System	Phase VII Retirement	Eliminated From	Eliminated To	Dismantled FY97-FY00	Nos. Dismantled FY90-FY97	1991 Declaration Commitment to Eliminate
Army (Marine Corps)							
W-70	Lance	FY92	February 92	Nov. 96		1,170	850
W-33	8in	FY92	?	?			500 at least
W-48	155mm	FY93	April 92	April 96		759	500 at least
W-79	8in		June 98[11]	FY2003	Y	3	~300?
Total Army						**1,932**	**2,150**
Navy							
B-57*	ND/SB	FY93	November 89	March 95		2,242	900 NDB
W-80-0	SLCM				Y		
Total Navy						**2,242**	**900 NDB**
Total Army + Navy						**4,174**	**3,050**
Air Force (Navy/Marine Corps*) Strike Bombs							
B-57	See Navy						
B61-2*	Bomb		June 96	March 97		1,159 all B61 mods	
B61-5*	Bomb		March 97	August 97			
B61-3, -4, -10	Bomb				Y		

The United States stocks of TNWs have also been consolidated. In general, according to the United States Department of Defense (DOD) "nuclear weapons storage locations have been reduced by over 75 percent", between 1988 and 1994.[12] Recent reductions and consolidations have included the reduction of Navy TNWs (SLCMs) storage sites from four to two:

- In the Atlantic: Naval Weapons Station Yorktown, VA, transferred its SLCMs to the Strategic Weapons Facility Atlantic in the Summer of 1997. The SLCMs are stored with Trident warheads near the King's Bay, GA, Trident SSBN base.[13]
- In the Pacific: NAS North Island, San Diego, CA, transferred its SLCMs to the Strategic Weapons Facility Pacific. They are stored with Trident warheads near the Bangor, WA, Trident SSBN base.[14]

Importantly, however, from the perspective of worries about forward-deployed TNWs, United States tactical nuclear weapons are thought to be kept at 10 bases in 7 European North Atlantic Treaty Organisation (NATO) countries.

Table 5 summarises the status of domestic and foreign United States TNW deployments.

Table 5

Number of US Nuclear Weapon Storage Sites 1985, 1992, 2001[15]			
	1985	1992	2001
Storage Sites			
Domestic	39	34	12
Overseas	125	16	10
Total	**164**	**50**	**22**
Number of US States with nuclear weapons		25	12
Number of US States with TNW			**4**
Europe—10 Bases in 7 Countries (B61 bombs) Kleine Brogel AB, Belgium; Buchel AB, Germany; Ramstein AB, Germany; Spangdahlem AB, Germany; Araxos AB, Greece; Aviano AB, Italy; Ghedi Authorization Bill, Italy; Vokel AB, The Netherlands; Incirlik AB, Turkey; RAF Lakenheath, UK			

Table 6 summarises the locations of United States TNWs before and after the 1991-92 declarations to show the large reduction in areas of deployment and to underscore some important withdrawals that represented key improvements in the security and safety of American TNWs and in crisis stability. Particularly noteworthy is the complete denuclearization of the Army, resulting in the removal and elimination of all Army TNWs—including the worrisome (from the perspective of security) nuclear artillery shells—from front-line locations in Europe and South Korea. Also, Navy TNWs were removed from warships and submarines afloat, from forward-deployed logistic surface ships such as the submarine tender in La Maddalena, Italy, and other forward-deployment locations such as Guam and Adak, Alaska, close to the Soviet Union. Finally, Air Force TNWs bombs also were removed from South Korea.

Table 6

US TNW Consolidation from 1991 to 2001[16]		
	1991 TNWs Locations	**2001**
Army/Marine Corps		
Lance	Europe, CA, NM, NY, TX	—
Artillery	Europe, Korea, CA, NM, NY, TX	—
Navy		
B-57 depth bomb	Europe, Pacific, AK, CA, FL, HI, ME, TX, VA	—
SLCMs	Europe (IT), Pacific (Guam), CA, HI, NJ, SC, VA	GA, WA
Air Force (Navy/Marine Corps*) Tactical Bombs		
B-57 bomb*	Europe, Pacific, NM, NV	—
B61-2* -5* bombs	Europe, Pacific, Korea, CA, FL, HI, NM, NV, VA	—
B61-3,-4,-10 bombs	Europe, Pacific, CA, FL, HI, NM, NV, VA	Europe, NV, NM

Another interesting indication of the withdrawal and elimination of United States TNWs is the number of nuclear weapons-certified units in the United States military. Every unit that has a nuclear-weapons mission of transporting, storing or firing a nuclear weapon must be certified to do so by its service and by the Department of Defense. Table 7 presents the number of nuclear-certified units per year from 1989 to 2000. After the 1991-92 declarations there was a dramatic drop in the number of nuclear-certified units in the United States military. With the removal and elimination of all nuclear weapons for ground forces, the Army and Marine Corps no longer had any nuclear-certified units. The removal of TNWs from the Navy also resulted in a large drop in the number of Navy nuclear-certified units. Those that remain are a combination of nuclear-powered ballistic missile submarines (SSBNs), nuclear storage facilities and perhaps some 20 nuclear-powered attack submarines (SSNs) that retain a nuclear SLCM capability. The Air Force was least affected by the declarations, but even so its number of nuclear-certified units has dropped by over half.

Table 7

Number of Nuclear Weapons Certified Units in the US Military by Service 1989-2000[17]

	Army	Navy	Air Force	Marines	Total
CY89	141	187	49	17	**394**
CY90	139	200	44	18	**401**
FY91	139	200	44	18	**401**
FY92	1	81	35	0	**117**
FY93	1	31	35	0	**67**
FY94	1	29	30	0	**60**
FY95	1	34	26	0	**61**
FY96	0	36	22	0	**58**
FY97	0	38	27	0	**65**
FY98	0	38	21	0	**59**
FY99	0	38	21	0	**59**
FY00	0	38	21	0	**59**

With respect to the Soviet Union or Russia, although there is not a lot of official data about the status of the implementation of the declarations, some interesting points can still be noted. Russian officials have elaborated about what the declarations include and by when Russia expected to have finished implementing them (as noted, the United States has not specified completion dates, but has provided more information about the types and numbers of TNWs affected by the declarations). Table 8 summarises this information.

Table 8

	Eliminated by	
Army[18]	**2000**	- All nuclear warheads on three types of shorter-range missiles
	2000	- All nuclear warheads for six types of artillery guns of 152mm, 203mm, and 240mm calibre
	1998	- All nuclear "mines"
Navy	**1995**[19] or *end of* **1996**[20]	- One-third
Air Force	By **1996** or *end of* **1997**	- One-half
Air Defence	By **1996** or *end of* **1996**	- One-half

The removal from deployment of TNWs, appears to have occurred relatively quickly in the case of the former Soviet republics.[21] Although official information is lacking, it also seems that TNWs were removed from Eastern Europe and Transcaucasus before the 1991 declarations, as shown in Table 9.[22]

Table 9

TNW Removals from Eastern Europe and Former Soviet Republics	
	Accomplished by
Central Asia/Kazakhstan/Baltic States	December 1991[23]
Ukraine	5-6 May 1992[24]
Belarus	Early 1992/Spring 1992[25]

In terms of removals by service, the data is more imprecise than in the case of the United States, but it appears Russia was not as quick as the United States to remove TNWs from deployment.

Table 10

TNW Removals from Armed Service	
	Accomplished by
Army	September 1997[26]
Navy Surface ships, submarines and land-based naval air	February 1993[27]
Air Defence	September 1996[28]

Some have worried that the apparent slow withdrawal of Russian TNWs represents the preservation of some TNWs capability above that was implied by Russian commitments made in the declaration. Yet, whatever residual TNWs capability may exist must be considered in the context of declining number of nuclear-capable platforms due to the break-up of Soviet Union and the accelerated retirement of platforms due to ageing and/or lack of maintenance. For example, the number of nuclear-capable ships in the Soviet/Russian Navy shrank from some 400 in 1990 to approximately 140 in 2001.[29]

In terms of elimination, Russia has not provided any detailed information comparable to that available from the United States. Of most concern, is that Russia seemingly had promised to finish the elimination of its ground forces nuclear weapons by 2000 or perhaps the end of 2000 (see Russian Foreign Minister Ivanov's statement to the Non-Proliferation Treaty (NPT) 2000 Review Conference footnoted below). As of September 2001, there had been no official confirmation that this had taken place. Table 11 summarises some official and semi-official statements about the status of the elimination of Russian TNWs.

Russian TNW storage sites have also been consolidated and reduced by over 250.[30] By 1996, the number of nuclear storage facilities declined to one-third of 1991 levels.[31] In November 1997, one Russian official noted that there were "80 protection areas around nuclear installations"[32] which needed mines for their defence. (In 2000, the United States Department of Defense was helping to improve facilities at 123 nuclear weapons storage sites, 23 Russian Strategic Missile Troops sites and 48 Navy and Air Force facilities.[33] Today, it is believed that the number of facilities/bases hosting

TNWs is a lot smaller.) The number of Russian nuclear weapons storage in depots is summarised in Table 12.

Table 11

Army	September 1996—being eliminated[34] December 1997—mines and TNW from FSU republics being eliminated[35] October 1998—being eliminated[36] November 1998—being eliminated[37] **April 2000—About to complete elimination**[38]
Navy	By June 1996—1/3 eliminated[39]
Air Force	By April 2000—1/2 eliminated
Air Defence	By June 1996—1/2 eliminated[40]

Table 12

Number of Nuclear Weapons Storage Facilities	**1990**	**1995**	**2001**	**With TNW**
Eastern Europe	Y	N	N	N
Soviet/Russian National Storage Sites	Y	Y	15	Y
ICBM bases	Y	Y	19+	N
Strategic Bomber bases	Y	Y	3	?
Air Force and Navy	Y	Y	30+	Y
Air Defence/Army	Y	?	N?	N?
Total	**500-600+**	**<100**[41]	**~67**[42]	**~45?**

Russian Air Force TNWs may be kept in storage sites such as the one near the Kholm Air Base near Arkhangelsk Northern Russia. If so, some Russian air-delivered TNWs nuclear weapons are neither "forward-deployed" next to aircraft on airstrips, nor kept at national-level storage sites, but at bunkers in vicinity of airfields.

CONCLUSIONS

Elimination—What Results and the Need for More Openness

An unofficial estimate of the number of American and Russian operational TNWs is provided in Table 13. Since 1991, there has indeed been a large reduction in the number of deployed TNWs.

Table 13

	1991[43]	2001[44]
Estimated US TNWs[45]		
Army/Marine Corps	3,040	0
Navy	1,150	320 SLCMs
Air Force	2,975	1,350 B-61 bombs
Air Defence	0	0
Total	**7,165**	**1,670**
Estimated Soviet/Russian TNWs		
Ground Forces	4,800-6,700	0
Navy	3,400-5,000	850
Air Force	4,000-7,000	1,540
Air Defence	2,800-3,000	1,200
Total	**15,000-21,700**	**3,590**

Although the United States has not provided comprehensive information about its own stockpile size and reductions, the United States. Defense Department has occasionally made public its estimate of the Russian nuclear stockpile (e.g., in December 2000, the Russian nuclear stockpile "was estimated to be well under 25,000 warheads, a reduction of over 11,000 warheads since 1992".[46] These estimates, however, contain a wide degree of latitude due to the lack of reliable information about the size of the Russian stockpile and the rate of Russian warhead dismantlements.

From the NGO perspective, confidence in the estimated number of Russian TNWs is lower than in that estimated for the United States. This is not because the United States has provided comprehensive official information about its number and types of TNWs. The United States is as secretive about this information as Russia. However, the amount of official and semi-official information made available about the United States military, its nuclear weapons, its nuclear weapons strategy, launching platforms, etc., since the dawn of the nuclear age over 50 years ago is vastly greater than that provided by the Soviet Union and Russia. Moreover, western non-government experts have been steadily examining this material for most of this time. The accumulation of information and knowledge, therefore, gives greater confidence in the estimates of American TNWs.

As in the case of United States, unwarranted Russian secrecy about its nuclear weapons stockpile could be a subject for discussion and resolution in a United Nations forum. The world community would be more assured about the success of the United States and Soviet/Russian declarations if the two countries were more forthcoming about the details of their implementation.

More openness on the part of the United States and Russia could substitute for more rigorous verification measures and underscore the utility of unilateral initiatives. Both the United States and Russia could give overall figures on their TNWs holdings in 1991 and presently. The United States, in particular, could provide more consistent information on the elimination and numbers of weapons eliminated and explain the discrepancies in the information released heretofore.

Russia, in turn, could provide more information on types of weapons eliminated and dismantled. Most importantly, Russia should confirm as soon as possible if it has finished destruction of ground forces weapons. Former Minister of Defense, Igor Sergeyev, and current advisor to President Putin, unfortunately refused to affirm that Russia had completed implementing its commitments under the declarations in his appearance at the Carnegie Endowment's annual Non-Proliferation conference in June 2001.[47]

Need to Solve the Reversibility Problem

The stockpile of nuclear warheads by the United States and Russian nuclear weapons production capacity suggest the potential for reversing the reduction in deployed TNWs at some point in the future. In the case of the United States, a good recent example of this problem is the B-61-10 bomb that was manufactured utilising the W85 warheads removed from the

Pershing II intermediate-range missiles eliminated under the 1987 INF Treaty.[48]

In addition to reducing TNWs, further agreements and methods should be developed to insure that TNW disarmament measures cannot easily be reversed. These steps should also extend to preventing a nuclear-capability to be restored to units that are no longer nuclear-certified.

Security of TNW

This has been a major concern of many analysts and commentators. It is frequently claimed that TNWs are somehow less securely stored than strategic nuclear weapons (SNWs) and thus special steps in dealing with TNW are warranted. However, one result of the 1991-92 declarations is that TNWs are approximately now as secure as SNWs. TNWs security is now as good or bad, and this is a large change from 1990-1991.[49] TNWs in the United States and Russia are in many cases co-located with SNWs in major nuclear weapons storage sites, with multiple bunkers. Moreover, major changes in deployments have improved the security situation for TNWs. There are almost no forwardly deployed or dispersed TNWs on land and there are no TNWs deployed on American or Russian ships or submarines. The only exception are the TNWs aircraft bombs the United States still bases in Europe which are now kept in vaults in hangers where aircraft are located. In the case of Russia, some TNWs may be located in storage areas in the vicinity of an airfield, but unlike the United States, they are not on the airfield area proper. Lastly, many of the supposedly smaller and more easily transportable TNW, such as artillery shells, may have been completely eliminated. Thus concerns about them being stolen are now (or soon to be) moot.

If a thief has the leisure to decide while stealing a nuclear weapon, there are several reasons why TNWs may not provide an attractive target for would-be thieves. In terms of general ease of theft, no modern nuclear weapon is terribly large. If a group could gain access to a storage bunker, a modest number of people could have the possibility to carry off any type of nuclear weapon. TNWs in a storage configuration may be as easy to carry off as SNWs under such circumstances. In terms of desirability, the obstacles to detonating a TNW which has been prepared for storage or retired may be the same or greater than for a SNW. Moreover, if the goal is to obtain fissile material, a SNW may contain more fissile material than a TNW. In terms of vulnerability, a major concern is the susceptibility of nuclear weapons to theft during transport. Today, there is perhaps even less logistical movement of TNWs than of SNWs. Moreover, SNWs may be more vulnerable as they are transported more often from remote base areas.

The Future of TNWs

The future of TNWs is uncertain. There are pressures to keep TNWs in United States and Russian arsenals as well as pressures to de-emphasise and reduce them.

TNWs are still seen as generally important, and the United States is determined to maintain its TNWs capability. The United States regularly holds nuclear SLCM regeneration exercises.[50] Moreover, American TNWs are deployed in Europe for political unity and new NATO missions. In addition, in the United States, the enthusiasm for stopping or countering the proliferation of weapons of mass-destruction—promoted both by arms controllers and hawks—is creating the political space and pressures for new missions for TNWs and new TNWs, i.e., the B61-11 Earth-penetrating bomb and discussion of need for new low-yield bombs.

From Russia there are news reports about the need for TNWs. These reports seemingly are based on the views of the same type of people who are advocating TNWs in the United States, hawks and people from the weapons laboratories. It does not seem to be official policy to acquire new types of TNWs—yet. Also, Russia, like the United States, maintains its TNWs preparedness. Of note, a Russian General described a Russian tactical nuclear weapons exercise in March and June 1999 that involved a "rocket brigade".[51] It is not clear if a ground or air unit was involved, since both could have "rockets". If it were the former, this news would be disturbing in light of Russia's pledge to denuclearize the Army; the denuclearization of the Army should have been almost completed in 1999. Moreover, there were news reports in January and February 2001 about Russian TNWs in Kaliningrad. If true, this may be an indication that Russia was exercising its allowed TNWs capability:[52] movement of TNWs to airbase storage or exercise thereof, or exercise by the Russian Navy similar to the United States (although, TNWs movement to or an exercise in Kaliningrad goes against Gorbachev-era pledge to denuclearize the Baltic).

There are, however, some pressures to further reduce and eliminate TNWs. American nuclear SLCMs could decrease due to the 11 September events as nuclear versions could be converted into conventional variants.[53] Also, there has been a bit of a debate in the submarine community over whether to keep SLCMs or give them up.[54] Finally, the American nuclear submarine force is over-extended[55] and some in the submarine community are concerned about the added burden of keeping a nuclear SLCMs capability.

In general, there may be a possibility to eliminate nuclear SLCMs. It was a lost opportunity that President Bush did not take up President Gorbachev's offer to get rid of all naval TNWs. Complete destruction of naval TNWs would have been a good disarmament step and further eased burden of verifying the declarations. However, there may be still some interest in the Russian Navy to eliminate nuclear SLCMs.

Either through unilateral steps or in conjunction with Russia, conceivably, the United States may end up with only aircraft-mounted TNWs, and thus have a "strategic" TNW arsenal.

Low-numbers of TNWs Preferable to Low-numbers of SNWs?

It may be premature to advocate the complete elimination of all TNWs. In fulfilling their NPT Article 6 commitments, a good way-station towards zero nuclear weapons may be to set aside a small number of air-delivered TNW bombs rather than keep low-levels of land- or sea-based SNWs.

A world of small numbers of TNWs would be as stable if not more so than a world of small numbers of SNWs. TNWs could be just as secure from attack and theft, even if they were dispersed to a few more locations. There would be less concern about hair-trigger alert launches and if launched, aircraft carrying TNWs could be recalled. There would be better C3 than with sea-based SNWs, and less worry about naval nuclear accidents. It would cost less to maintain some dual-capable aircraft (or bombers in general) for carrying TNWs than SNWs and their bases. In the case of the United States, the overhead for maintaining a separate nuclear command, STRATCOM, could be eliminated.

In essence, the idea would be to return to a world of a few nuclear-capable bombers. At this point, equivalent force structures may facilitate the final steps towards zero. It could be easier to obtain the final reductions if bomber weapons were balanced against bomber weapons, rather than to try to balance trade-off between different kinds of SNWs, especially if each country decides to keep a different mixture of forces.

Endnotes

* The author would like to thank the Ploughshares Foundation and the John Merck Fund in conjunction with the Natural Resources Defense Council for support research involving satellite imagery.

1. In terms of the choice by the United States of which TNWs to include in its declaration, the historical context was important. Brent Scowcroft, National Security Advisor to President George Bush, wrote in his joint memoir that: the reunification of Germany made short-range TNW "undesirable"; South Korea was suggesting the removal of United States TNWs; "a number of countries", including Japan and New Zealand, had problems with the United States Navy carrying nuclear weapons into their ports and the United States policy of neither confirming nor denying the presence of nuclear weapons on its ships; and, finally, nuclear Anti-Submarine Weapons (ASW) were no longer the "preferred" way to attack submarines. As a result, he then recommended that the United States get rid of all its TNWs except air-delivered ones. See George Bush and Brent Scrowcroft, *A World Transformed*, Knopf, 1998, pp. 536-547.

   In regards to naval TNWs, this is an interesting frank admission by a high policy-maker that public protests (of which there were many in the 1980s against American nuclear-capable and armed vessels) and foreign concerns led directly to their withdrawal and the elimination of most.

   For more on the genesis of President Bush's 27 September proposals see: John E. Yang, "Bush Plan Emerged After Failed Coup: White House Wanted to Take Advantage of Timing, Officials Say", *The Washington Post*, 28 September 1991; Andrew Rosenthal, "Bush's Arms Plan: Arms Plan Germinated in Back-Porch Session", *The New York Times*, 29 September 1991; Doyle McManus, "Bush Acted to Help Gorbachev Control A-Arms", *The Los Angeles Times*, 29

September 1991; Michael Beschloss and Strobe Talbott, *At the Highest Levels*, Little Brown, 1993; Colin L. Powell, *My American Journey*, Ballentine, 1995 and James Baker, *The Politics of Diplomacy*, Putnam, 1995.

For Gorbachev's reaction see: interview with Gorbachev, "Gorbachev-Bush Proposals 'A Serious Advance Towards a Nonnuclear World'", *Central Television, First All Union Programme*, 28 September 1991. For background on Gorbachev's reaction, see Pavel Palazchenko's description of the initial response of Gorbachev and his advisors; Pavel Palazchenko, *My Years with Gorbachev and Shevardnadze*, The Pennsylvania State University Press, 1997. Also, one of Gorbachev's key advisors, Anatoly Chernyaev mentions the Kremlin's positive reaction with respect to strategic nuclear weapons, saying Gorbachev's response to Bush did not meet with the "usual resistance and delays on the part of the military"; Anatoly Chernyaev, *My Six Years with Gorbachev*, English and Tucker, trans, The Pennsylvania State University Press, 1997.

2. Defense Secretary Dick Cheney, Chairman of the Joint Chiefs of Staff General Colin Powell, "Defense Department Briefing: Details of President Bush's Arms Proposal", 27 September 1991; Pete Williams, "Defense Department Briefing", 1 October 1991; T. Cochran et al., *US Nuclear Forces and Capabilities, Nuclear Weapons Databook, Volume I*, Ballinger, 1984; Natural Resources Defense Council (NRDC) Nuclear Notebook, "US Nuclear Weapons Stockpile", *Bulletin of the Atomic Scientists*, June 1991 and June 1992.
3. President George Bush, "New Initiatives to Reduce US Nuclear Forces", *US Department of State Dispatch*, 30 September 1991, Vol. 2, No. 39; US Department of Defense, "DOD Review Recommends Reduction in Nuclear Forces", Press Release and accompanying "Nuclear Posture Review" briefing, 22 September 1994.
4. M. S. Gorbachev, "Gorbachev Proposals on Nuclear Arms Control", *Central Television, First All Union Programme*, 5 October 1991; President Yeltsin's Disarmament Statement, 29 January 1992, *Moscow Teleradiokompaniya Ostankino Television First Program Network*, 29 January 1992; "Boris Yeltsin's Statement on Arms Control", *ITAR-TASS*, 29 January 1992.
5. In addition to sources cited in elimination section below, see: Andrew Weston-Dawkes, "Enduring Stockpile—1998", United States Department of Energy (DOE), Office of Declassification, 2 October

1998, fax, released under the Freedom of Information Act (FOIA) to Princeton University's Program on Science and Global Security (PSGS).

6. "Today I can tell you that all of the planned withdrawals are complete. All ground-launched tactical nuclear weapons have been returned to US territory, as have all naval tactical nuclear weapons. Those weapons designated to be destroyed are being retired and scheduled for destruction", President George Bush, "Statement on the United States Nuclear Weapons Initiative", 2 July 1992.
   According to the United States Air Force's 6th Airlift Squadron history, the removal of United States nuclear weapons from Europe during 1991-92, was "the largest nuclear weapons movement in United States' history". The 6th Airlift Squadron conducted Prime Nuclear Airlift Force (PNAF) missions, i.e., it had the main responsibility for airlifting United States nuclear weapons to and from Europe, while based at McGuire AFB, NJ. Over 1,600 PNAF missions were conducted between 1971 and 1993; McGuire AFB website, downloaded 8 November 2000.
7. South Korean President Roh Tae Woo announced on national television that no nuclear weapons were now in South Korea; James Sterngold, "Seoul Says It Now Has No Nuclear Arms", *The New York Times*, 19 December 1991.
8. "No nuclear weapons remain in the custody of US ground forces", United States Department of Defense; "DOD Review Recommends Reduction in Nuclear Forces", Press Release and accompanying "Nuclear Posture Review" briefing, 22 September 1994.
9. "On the basis of President Bush's 1991 Nuclear Initiative, NATO took the decision to reduce the number of nuclear weapons available for its sub-strategic forces in Europe by over 85 percent. These reductions were completed in 1993", Press Release M-DPC/NPG-1(2001)87; "Final Communiqué: Ministerial Meeting of the Defence Planning Committee and the Nuclear Planning Group", 7 June 2001.
10. C. Bruce Tarter, Director, University of California, Lawrence Livermore National Laboratory, "The Department of Energy's Budget Request for FY 1998", Hearing of the Subcommittee on Strategic Forces Committee on Armed Services United States Senate, 19 March 1997; United States Department of Energy, "Nuclear Weapons Disassembly (by Weapons Program) at Pantex Plant", "Pantex Plant Nuclear Weapons Disassembly History by Weapons System", "Nuclear Warhead Dismantlement 1997-1999 and 2000", and "Retired/

Cancelled Weapons", all released under the Freedom of Information Act or from DOE Public Affairs to Princeton University's PSGS.

11. *US Defense Nuclear Facilities Safety Board, Tenth Annual Report to Congress*, February 2000. According to this report there were "many difficulties encountered by DOE while readying the W79 for dismantlement". Also see John Gordon, Under-Secretary for Nuclear Security and Administrator, National Nuclear Security Administration, US Energy Department, Statement before the Senate Appropriations Subcommittee on Energy and Water Development, 26 April 2001.
12. United States Department of Defense, "DOD Review Recommends Reduction in Nuclear Forces", Press Release and accompanying "Nuclear Posture Review" briefing, 22 September 1994.
13. Naval Surface Warfare Center, Indian Head Division, Detachment McAlester, "War Reserve Weapons Maintenance and Logistics: Nuclear Weapons Consolidation", *Navy Nuclear Weapons Digest*, Third/Fourth Quarters 1997; released under the Freedom of Information Act to Princeton University's PSGS.
14. E.g. Director, Strategic Systems Programs, "Completion Inspection at Strategic Weapons Facility Pacific", Letter 5 March 1998 to the Chief of Naval Operations (N41), released under the Freedom of Information Act to Princeton University's PSGS.
15. William Arkin and Richard Fieldhouse, *Nuclear Battlefields: Global Links in the Arms Race*, Ballinger,1985; Greenpeace/NRDC, *Taking Stock: US Nuclear Deployments at the End of the Cold War*, 1992; William Arkin, Robert Norris, Joshua Handler, *Taking Stock: Worldwide Nuclear Deployments, 1998*, NRDC, March 1998; Hans Kristensen and Joshua Handler, "Appendix 6A. Tables of Nuclear Forces", *SIPRI Yearbook 2001*, 2001; Electronic Systems Center, Hanscom AFB, "WS3 (Weapons Storage and Security System) Sustainment Program", Program Management Review Briefing for USAFE LG, 3 March 2000, released under the Freedom of Information Act to Princeton University's PSGS.
16. William Arkin and Richard Fieldhouse, *Nuclear Battlefields: Global Links in the Arms Race*; Greenpeace/NRDC, *Taking Stock: US Nuclear Deployments at the End of the Cold War*; William Arkin, Robert Norris, Joshua Handler, *Taking Stock: Worldwide Nuclear Deployments, 1998*; Hans Kristensen and Joshua Handler, "Appendix 6A. Tables of Nuclear Forces", *SIPRI Yearbook 2001*; Electronic Systems Center, Hanscom AFB, "WS3 (Weapons Storage and Security System) Sustainment Program".

17. Information obtained under the Freedom of Information Act from the Defense Special Weapons Agency (DSWA) and from United States Defense Department's Defense Threat Reduction Agency Public Affairs by Princeton's PSGS.
18. Vladimir Lobov, Gen. of the Army, "The Motherland's Armed Forces Today and Tomorrow", *Krasnaya Zvezda*, 29 November 1991; Gen. Vitally Yakovlev, "Realization of Reduction and Limitation Programs for Nuclear Weapons and the Opportunity of an Information Exchange on Amount of Produced Fissile Materials and Their Localization", talk prepared for the United States-Russian Workshop on Comprehensive Test Ban, Fissile Material Cutoff and Plutonium Disposal, 15-17 December 1993, Washington, DC, Natural Resources Defense Council, Federation of American Scientists, Moscow Physical-Technical Institute.
19. Vladimir Lobov, Gen. of the Army, "The Motherland's Armed Forces Today and Tomorrow"; Gen. Vitally Yakovlev, Talk Prepared for the United States-Russian Workshop of CTB, Fissile Material Cutoff and Plutonium Disposal.
20. United States Department of Defense, *Proliferation: Threat and Response*, November 1997, p. 44.
21. In addition to sources cited below, for a lengthier review of Soviet TNW removals from Eastern Europe and the Former Soviet Republics see Joshua Handler, *Russian Nuclear Warhead Dismantlement Rates and Storage Site Capacity: Implications for the Implementation of START II and De-Alerting Initiatives,* CEES Report No. AC-99-0, 1999. Note that it remains unclear if Soviet TNWs were deployed in Bulgaria.
22. From 1990 to 1991 all TNWs were removed from the former Warsaw Pact countries with the last train "loaded with tactical warheads" leaving Germany during the summer of 1991; Gen. Vitally Yakovlev, United States-Russian Workshop on Comprehensive Test Ban, Fissile Material Cutoff and Plutonium. Lt. Gen. Vladimir Korotkov, deputy chief of the Main Department of the Commonwealth of Independent States (CIS) Armed Forces, said all nuclear weapons were removed from the Transcaucasian republics in the Summer of 1990; "General: No Nuclear Arms in Caucasus", *Interfax*, 12 March 1992.
23. In 1992, Gen. Zelentsov of the 12th Main Directorate of the Russian Ministry of Defence said that there were "no tactical nuclear weapons in the Central Asian republics or in Kazakhstan. The last warhead had been withdrawn from their territories last year"; Victor Litovkin, "Generals in Moscow Categorically Deny Sales of Nuclear Weapons",

Izvestia, 17 March 1992; Gen. Zelentsov said that, "The process of the transfer of tactical nuclear weapons from other CIS states began as early as last year [1991]. Gradually their numbers were reduced and they were evacuated first from the states which are the farthest from Russia. Their number has gradually decreased as they were withdrawn first from the countries that are geographically most distant from Russia, and then from the countries that are closer to it"; Press Conference on Withdrawal of Tactical Nuclear Weapons from the Ukraine by Members of CIS and Ukraine Military, Official Kremlin International News Broadcast, 6 May 1992 (Federal News Service). Gen. Gely Batenin, an advisor to the Russian Foreign Ministry said that all TNWs had been removed from the Baltic States, Transcaucasia, and Central Asia; Alexander Rahr, "Batenin on Nuclear Weapons", *RFE/RL*, No. 236, 13 December 1991.

24. Gen. Zelentsov said: "They [TNWs] were withdrawn from Belarus some time ago, and from Ukrainian territory they were pulled out, in fact, yesterday. To be more exact, it happened last night". Gen. Yakovlev added that in the "course of the last transfer, some 1,000 nuclear units have been evacuated—tactical nuclear weapons". These were mostly air defence weapons, tactical aviation bombs, and naval tactical weapons; Press Conference on Withdrawal of Tactical Nuclear Weapons from the Ukraine by Members of CIS and Ukraine Military.
25. Mikhail Shimansky, "First Interview with First Defense Minister of Byelarus", *Izvestia*, 24 April 1992.
26. "All the warheads of the ground forces, artillery shells and tactical nuclear warheads, have been removed and the units which maintained nuclear warheads have been disbanded"; Press Conference with Lt. Gen. Igor Valynkin, Chief of the 12th Main Directorate of the Russian Ministry of Defense, regarding the nuclear security in Russian Federation armed forces, Russian Ministry of Defense, Official Kremlin International News Broadcast, 25 September 1997 (Federal News Service).
27. "All tactical nuclear weapons have been removed from vessels, multi-purpose submarines, and aircraft of the naval forces, and placed in centralized storage". Information from the Russian Ministry of Defense reported in Vadim Byrkin, "Tactical Nuclear Weapons Removed from Vessels", *ITAR-TASS* World Service, 4 February 1993.
28. Foreign Ministry spokesman Mikhail Demurin reportedly said that, "The nuclear warheads of anti-aircraft missiles have been withdrawn".

"Disarmament Initiatives to be Fulfilled by Year 2000", *Interfax*, 26 September 1996.

29. Hans Kristensen and Joshua Handler, "Appendix 6A. Tables of Nuclear Forces", *SIPRI Yearbook 2001*.
30. Col. Gen. Yevgeny Maslin, "Summary of the Proceedings of the US Defense Nuclear Agency's 4th Annual International Conference on Controlling Arms", Philadelphia, PA, 19-22 June 1995.
31. Col. Gen. Yevgeny Maslin, "Cooperative Threat Reduction: The View from Russia", in *Proceedings of the NATO Advanced Research Workshop on Dismantlement and Destruction of Chemical, Nuclear and Conventional Weapons, Bonn, Germany, 19-21 May 1996*, Dordrecht: Kluwer Academic Publishers, The Netherlands, 1997; Col. Gen. Yevgeny Maslin, "Walking the Walk: Controlling Arms in the 1990s".
32. "Sergeyev on Use of Russian 'Suitcase' Nuclear Weapons", *Interfax*, 15 November 1997.
33. "USA Installing Automated Nuclear Weapons Monitoring System in Russia", *ITAR-TASS*, 5 December 2000.
34. "Disarmament Initiatives to be Fulfilled by Year 2000", *Interfax*, 26 September 1996.
35. By December 1997, Gen. Valynkin said that 60 percent of the TNWs removed from the Ukraine, Byelorussia and Kazakhstan had been destroyed. Moreover, mines would be destroyed by the year 2000; Vladimir Georgiev, Igor Frolov, "A Storm in a Bottle", *Nezavisimaya Gazeta*, 12 December 1997.
36. Mikhail Shevtsov, "Russia Strictly Fulfilling Nuclear Test Ban Treaty", *ITAR-TASS*, 9 October 1998. Gen. Valynkin in an interview noted that the elimination of "expired nuclear weapons" was on going and nuclear mines and shells were also being dismantled; Vladimir Karpenko, "Emergency Situations Will Never Occur at Nuclear Facilities Thanks to Special Security Regime", *Rossiiskiye Vesti*, 28 October 1998.
37. [Interviewer] "Do the Missile and Artillery Troops remain a means of employing tactical nuclear weapons?" [Mukhin] "The Missile and Artillery Troops still remain a means of employing them. But in today's conditions, when there is a gradual elimination of tactical nuclear weapons going on, we no longer have them in storage". Sergey Sokut, interview with Lt. Gen. Nikolay Mukhin, Deputy Chief of the Missile and Artillery Troops of the RF Armed Forces, "The Primary Weapon to Defeat the Enemy: That Is How Lt-Gen Nikolay Mukhin, Deputy Chief

of the Missile and Artillery Troops of the RF Armed Forces Characterizes the Role of the 'God of War'", *Nezavisimoye Voyennoye Obozreniye*, 13-19 November 1998.

38. "Russia also continues to consistently implement its unilateral initiatives related to tactical nuclear weapons. Such weapons have been completely removed from surface ships and multipurpose submarines, as well as from the land-based naval aircraft, and are stored at centralized storage facilities. One third of all nuclear munitions for the sea-based tactical missiles and naval aircraft has been eliminated. We are about to complete the destruction of nuclear warheads from tactical missiles, artillery shells and nuclear mines. We have destroyed half of the nuclear warheads for anti-aircraft missiles and for nuclear gravity bombs". Igor S. Ivanov, Minister of Foreign Affairs of the Russian Federation, Statement at the Review Conference of the Parties to the Treaty on the Non-Proliferation of Nuclear Weapons, New York, 25 April 2000.
39. Col. Gen. Yevgeny Maslin remarks on United States and Russian Perspectives on the Cooperative Threat Reduction Program, made at the United States Defense Special Weapons Agency conference, "Walking the Walk: Controlling Arms in the 1990s", in "Summary of the Fifth Annual International Conference on Controlling Arms", Norfolk, VA, 3-6 June 1996.
40. Yevgeny Maslin, "Walking the Walk: Controlling Arms in the 1990s".
41. John Deutch, Director, Central Intelligence, statement before the Senate Permanent Subcommittee on Investigations, hearing on Global Proliferation of Weapons of Mass Destruction, Part II, 22 March 1996, Senate Hearing, Part. II; Gordon Oehler, Director, Non-Proliferation Center, CIA, testimony before the Senate Armed Services Committee, on Intelligence Briefing on Smuggling of Nuclear Material and the Role of International Crime Organizations, and on the Proliferation of Cruise and Ballistic Missiles, 31 January 1995; Gloria Duffy, testimony before the House Foreign Affairs Committee, Subcommittee on Europe and the Middle East, Hearings on FY 1995 Foreign Aid Requests for Russia and the Other New Independent States (NIS) of the Former Soviet Union, 24 March 1994; United States Department of Defense, *Proliferation: Threat and Response*, November 1997.
42. For analysis of the Russian nuclear weapons storage system see Joshua Handler, "Lifting the Lid on Russia's Nuclear Weapons Storage", *Jane's Intelligence Review*, August 1999.

43. Robert Norris and William Arkin, "US Nuclear Weapons Stockpile", *Bulletin of the Atomic Scientists*, June 1991 and June 1992, and "Nuclear Notebook: Estimated Soviet Nuclear Stockpile (July 1991)", *Bulletin of the Atomic Scientists*, July/August 1991; Alexei Arbatov, "Deep Cuts and De-alerting: A Russian Perspective" in Harold Feivson (ed.), *The Nuclear Turning Point: A Blueprint for Deep Cuts and De-Alerting of Nuclear Weapons*, Washington, DC: Brookings, 1999.
44. Hans Kristensen and Joshua Handler, "Appendix 6A. Tables of Nuclear Forces", *SIPRI Yearbook 2001*.
45. Of note, Ambassador Robert Grey informed the 2000 NPT Review Conference that "The US has reduced its non-strategic nuclear weapons by 80 percent since the fall of the Berlin Wall"; United States Ambassador Robert Grey, Statement to the Main Committee I, The 2000 Review Conference of the Treaty on Non-Proliferation of Nuclear Weapons, 27 April 2000.
46. United States Department of Defense, *Proliferation: Threat and Response*, January 2001.
47. http://www.ceip.org/files/projects/npp/resources/Conference%202001/sergeyev.htm
48. Robert Norris and William Arkin, "Beating Swords into Swords", *The Bulletin of the Atomic Scientists*, November 1990.
49. Despite the many concerns raised since 1989-90 about the security of Soviet TNWs, the Soviet and then Russian military has consistently denied reports that any nuclear weapons are missing and that nuclear weapons in storage are insecure. The only attempt to filch a Soviet TNW about which any details are known was made by the environmental group Greenpeace. In the summer of 1991, Greenpeace tried to "borrow" a Soviet nuclear weapon from its storage site in East Germany in order to show it to the world's press for an anti-nuclear weapons protest in Berlin. The weapon was to be returned after the action. The plan fell apart when the remaining Soviet nuclear weapons were removed from East Germany in July-August 1991. See William Burrows and Robert Windrem, *Critical Mass: The Dangerous Race for Superweapons in a Fragmenting World*, Simon and Schuster, 1994, pp. 246-251.
50. Twice a year, the Navy selects an attack submarine for a "regeneration" exercise to evaluate the ability to re-deploy nuclear armed-cruise missiles on submarines. The exercise tests the ability of the crew to re-establish nuclear capability in a "relatively short time"; United States

Office of the Secretary of Defense, *Nuclear Weapons Systems Sustainment Programs,* May 1997.

51. Interview with General Igor Valynkin, Head of the 12th GUMO by Alexander Dolinin and Nikolai Poroskov, "The Nuclear Genie of Russia Sleeps", *Krasnaya Zvezda*, 31 August 1999.
52. Bill Gertz, "Satellites Pinpoint Russian Nuclear Arms in Baltics", *The Washington Times*, 15 February 2001.
53. "In addition to accelerating the acquisition of Tactical Tomahawk, the Navy also wants Raytheon to begin remanufacturing in 'large numbers' the nuclear-tipped TLAM-Ns, which have been in storage and out of the deployment arsenal since the early 1990s". Hunter Keeter, "PGM Funding May Top List for Short-Term Military Spending Increase", *Defense Daily*, 20 September 2001.
54. Capt. William Norris (Ret.), "What is TLAM/N and Why Do We Need It?", Lt. Michael Kostiuk, "Removal of the Nuclear Strike Option from United States Attack Submarines", and LCDR David DiOrio, USSTRATCOM, "The Role of Nuclear Sea-Launched Cruise Missiles in the Post Cold War Strategy", all in *The Submarine Review*, January 1998; Capt. Howard Venezia (Ret.), "The Sub Launched Nuclear Cruise Missile Debate", letter in *The Submarine Review*, April 1998.
55. For instance see Rear Admiral Albert H. Konetzni, United States Navy Commander, Submarine Force United States Pacific Fleet, Statement before the House Armed Services Committee Procurement Subcommittee Submarine Force Structure and Modernization Plans Hearing, 27 June 2000.

Part III

Nuclear Weapons Development and Testing

CHAPTER 12

NEW NUCLEAR WEAPONS DEVELOPMENT AND TESTING

Rebecca Johnson

INTRODUCTION

For much of the past decade, discussion of tactical nuclear weapons (TNWs) has tended to focus primarily on the 1991 Bush-Gorbachev declarations and the problems posed by Cold War TNWs, and particularly the Russian stockpiles. During the 1990s, the United States, Britain and France withdrew almost all their TNWs from Europe, dismantling whole classes of weapons. As is clear from the points made by some of the other chapters in the volume, however, concern is growing that the United States, in particular, may seek to develop and test new tactical nuclear weapons, specifically a low yield, deep penetrating warhead.

During the final year of negotiations of the Comprehensive Test Ban Treaty (CTBT), the United States promised that the zero yield test ban would preclude a host of new nuclear weapons. As a reminder, this is what the Arms Control and Disarmament affairs (ACDA) Director John Holum told the first Conference on Disarmament (CD) plenary of 1996:

> Without nuclear testing the nuclear weapon states will not be able to pursue confidently such technologies as the nuclear-explosion-pumped X-ray laser, the so-called nuclear shotgun, enhanced electromagnetic pulse weapons, microwave weapons and enhanced-radiation weapons... The true zero test ban will also place out of reach new "mini-nuke" and "micro-nuke" concepts—technologies designed to use nuclear explosive yields in small amounts... By fending off such developments, the CTBT will help make nuclear war less likely, and

sustain today's trend toward smaller nuclear arsenals with shrinking roles in national defences.[1]

Despite the promise of the zero yield test ban to halt the development of new nuclear weapons, however, through laboratory research and testing, including sub-critical tests, the United States has developed a modified version of the B-61 gravity bomb (the B-61-mod 11), to penetrate deeper into the ground. Now the laboratories and some of their supporters in the Pentagon and Congress want to go further.

In 1993-94, Congressional legislation, accepted by both the Pentagon, in the Nuclear Posture Review, and President Clinton, led to the United States laboratories being barred from developing precision, low yield nuclear weapons. In recent years, however, these positions have been undermined. The Warner-Allard provision of the FY2001 Senate Defense Authorization Bill partially overturned the 1993 legislation and required that the Department of Energy (DoE) do research and development work on "mini-nukes".

The price tag for the Clinton administration to take the zero yield decision on the CTBT consisted of six "safeguards" announced at the same time: a "Science-based stockpile stewardship" programme; maintenance of the nuclear weapon laboratories; a basic capability to resume testing if required; continuation of treaty-monitoring research and development; enhanced intelligence gathering; and the interpretation that "supreme national interests" could permit withdrawal from the treaty if the President, in consultation with Congress deemed testing necessary for maintaining the American "nuclear deterrent". Russia, Britain and France followed with similar conditions.

The United States has devoted more than $4 billion per year to the stockpile stewardship programme, which includes "sub-critical" tests, using the Nevada Test Site, and the National Ignition Facility (NIF) at the Lawrence Livermore National Laboratory, where inertial confinement fusion (ICF) experiments are underway. Los Alamos has the Dual Axis Radiographic Hydrotest (DARHT) facility in process and there are continuing plans for an Advanced Hydrotest Facility at the Nevada site.[2] France has the Laser Mégajoule facility for inertial confinement fusion tests, but less is known about the programmes and facilities of the other nuclear-weapon States that would be capable of designing new TNWs.

When it accepted the zero yield decision in May 1996, Russia spoke of stockpile management in terms almost identical with the United States. MinAtom subsequently procured supercomputer technology from the United States for Arzamas-16 and Chelyabinsk-70, despite American attempts to pull out of a deal that Moscow thought had been promised when Yeltsin agreed to the zero yield decision. Like the United States, Russia wants to use and maintain its remaining underground test site for sub-critical tests and other experiments, in part as an insurance against break-out, should the test ban or non-proliferation regime fail. But Russian officials acknowledge that they lag far behind the United States in funds and facilities.

The safeguards and stockpile programmes were treated by the nuclear-weapon States as essential for securing domestic agreement on the zero-yield CTBT, though they went far further than the non-nuclear weapon States had envisaged. For them, the CTBT was intended to place a cap on nuclear research and development, whereas the stockpile programmes appeared to be intended to circumvent this basic objective.

In statements to the CD, the United Nations General Assembly and First Committee in 1995 and 1996, several countries, notably India and Pakistan, repeatedly raised concerns about how much modernisation and qualitative improvement would be possible if the nuclear-weapon States took a mechanistic view of the CTBT and sought to replace what they were giving up under the treaty by testing with high-tech research facilities in the laboratories. India and Pakistan made clear that the credibility of the CTBT rested in part on how it affected vertical as well as horizontal proliferation, but their criticisms were dismissed as self-serving, as indeed they may to some extent have been.

Nevertheless, one former nuclear weapon designer, Richard Garwin, said in 1993 that "a reliable stockpile of nuclear weapons identical to those that we plan to keep in the inventory after 1996 can be maintained for many decades by the same kind of sampling and non-nuclear testing and remanufacturing that we practise now".[3] Other American nuclear scientists supported the view that an "engineering-based" stockpile stewardship programme was adequate for maintaining the ten warhead designs the United States intended to keep in its stockpile.[4]

Kortunov made the same point with respect to the Russian arsenal: "Stockpile confidence could be maintained without nuclear testing, by continuing to disassemble sample warheads, inspecting them for evidence of deterioration, and non-nuclear testing of the components. The non-nuclear tests include imploding instrumented primaries after the fissile material is replaced by inert material and following the progression of the implosion with fast X-ray cameras. Indeed, these procedures lie at the heart both of the Russian and American reliability testing programmes today".[5]

An engineering approach would have relied on warhead surveillance, computer simulation, chemical experiments, and laboratory experiments on weapon components to monitor ageing, ensure safety and provide confidence.[6] It would not require sub-critical experiments, the National Ignition Facility, DARHT or much else of the expensive paraphernalia and high tech shopping list in the United States stockpile stewardship programme. But the engineering approach to stockpile safety would have required that the nuclear weapon States rule out modifying, redesigning or significantly improving their nuclear weapons.

WHAT IS THE CURRENT SITUATION?

The CTBT is trapped in limbo, in large part due its overly stringent entry-into-force provision, compounded by the United States Senate's rejection in 1999 and the nuclear tests by India and Pakistan in May 1998. The United States now has "stockpile life extension programmes" (SLEPs), intended for modifications and possible new designs of nuclear weapons and the FY2002 budget allocates $5.3 billion for the National Nuclear Security Administration (NNSA), which now implements the stockpile stewardship programme.

Paul Robinson, Director of Sandia National Laboratories, argued in a paper entitled "Maintaining a viable nuclear weapon programme in a test ban environment" [March 2000] that: "The United States will undoubtedly require a new nuclear weapon, either for a different delivery mode or vehicle, or, quite likely, because it is realised that the yields of the weapons left over from the Cold War are too high for addressing the deterrence requirements of a multipolar, widely proliferated world". As the Warner-Allard provision demonstrated, Robinson and others have persuaded some Congressional leaders that they *should* want mini-nukes (by which they seem to mean weapons with yields of 5 kilotons or below) for use against hardened, deeply buried targets such as missile silos, chemical and biological weapons (CBW) stockpiles or a terrorist/"rogue"government command bunker.

In a further interview, actually published on 11 September 2001, Robinson argued even more explicitly: "Where the hell are we going to use missiles with four to eight warheads, or half-megaton yields? Even the few "tactical" nuclear weapons that we have have high yields of above 100 kilotons. I would hope the United States President would think it was crazy to use such weapons in response to a rogue-state attack. After a decade of trying to sort out what we learned from the Cold War and how we might fit our nuclear deterrence and deterrent message to fit the future, I now argue that we need lower-yield nuclear weapons that could hold at risk only a rogue State's leadership and tools of aggression with some degree of confidence.[7]

After the appalling attacks on the World Trade Center, the *Washington Times* published a piece from Thomas Woodrow, who resigned from the Defense Intelligence Agency (DIA) in May this year, after 22 years service as a United States intelligence officer. Woodrow, in what is widely viewed as flying a kite on behalf of interests high in the Pentagon, argued in favour of the use of nuclear weapons in Afghanistan: "The time has come for the United States to make good its past pledges that it will use all military capabilities at its disposal to defend US soil by delivering nuclear strikes against the instigators and perpetrators of the attacks". At a bare minimum, tactical nuclear capabilities should be used against the Bin Laden camps in the desert of Afghanistan. ... A series of low-level, tactical nuclear strikes in the Afghanistan desert would pose no risk to large population centres and would carry little risk of fallout spreading to populated areas. Also, our nuclear capabilities were designed to include such a mission, and they are capable of fulfilling such a mission. Lastly, the use of nuclear weapons against the Bin Laden groups and his supporters will rightly shock the world, but it will also shock those nations that have been disposed for a variety of reasons to back the terrorist groups with economic and political support".[8]

Woodrow's case that TNWs be used by America to "exterminate" (his word, not mine) Bin Laden and his supporters rested on three planks: 1) that not to use TNWs would be viewed as cowardice; 2) that a series of low level, tactical nuclear strikes would pose virtually no risk to civilians and population centres; and 3) that use of such nuclear weapons by the United States now would deter other would-be terrorist attackers. In effect, he was saying you can't use big nuclear weapons, but if you can't use tactical nuclear weapons now, in response to the 11 September attacks, whenever would you use nuclear weapons?

Viewed through a pinhole of military utility, Woodrow's first two arguments have some logic. What he, Robinson, and other advocates of developing more usable mini-nukes are missing is the point that for most people, a nuke is a nuke is a nuke. However small or surgically targeted, use of a mini-nuke crosses the nuclear threshold just as surely as an intercontinental ballistic missile. Woodrow and Robinson are right that this threshold dividing nuclear weapons use from conventional weapons acts as a self-deterrent—with good reason. For instance, what is thought of as deep penetrating TNWs will not penetrate deeply enough for the blast effects and radiation to be significantly contained. If a TNW is used, people won't notice whether or not it was small: what will matter is that the taboo on the use of nuclear weapons since 1945 will have been breached. That will turn world attention away from the culpability of the World Trade Center terrorists towards condemnation of the United States government for unleashing nuclear terror. If the current stockpiles of nuclear weapons are unusable, the answer is not to develop new, more usable types of weapons, but to work at eliminating nuclear weapons altogether, as mandated by international agreements, most notably the Non-Proliferation Treaty (NPT).

CONCLUSION

There are three central points that run through this entire volume and that bare emphasis:

1. There is an increasingly blurred distinction between tactical, sub-strategic, non-strategic and strategic nuclear weapons. During the Cold War, demarcations were made in terms of yield or range, but that will not work now, and we have to consider the questions of definition and function again.

2. While advocating the implementation of the 1991/92 declarations, we need to be clear that as long as new nuclear weapons—especially TNWs—are still being researched, developed or even just discussed as

possible future developments, particularly by the United States, addressing the security and elimination of Russia's existing TNWs will be very much harder.

3. The fate of the CTBT and the NPT have, from their inception, been inextricably intertwined. Playing fast and loose with the CTBT, as the United States is now doing, could lead to the collapse of that treaty and a resumption of nuclear testing. That in turn could lead to a further erosion of confidence in the NPT, with negative consequences for United States and international security.

Endnotes

1. John Holum, CD/PV.721, 23 January 1996.
2. Katherine Magraw, "The United States", in Eric Arnett (ed.), *Nuclear Weapons After the Comprehensive Test Ban*, SIPRI: Stockholm, 1996, pp. 116-128.
3. Richard L. Garwin, "Atoms do not age", *The Bulletin of the Atomic Scientists*, October 1993.
4. Katherine Magraw, "The United States".
5. Sergey V. Kortunov, "Russia", in Eric Arnett (ed.), *Nuclear Weapons After the Comprehensive Test Ban*, SIPRI: Stockholm, 1996, p. 94.
6. Katherine Magraw, "The United States".
7. "National lab director makes the case for new nukes", *Government Executive Magazine*, 11 September 2001.
8. Thomas Woodrow, "Time to use the nuclear option", *Washington Times*, 14 September 2001.

CHAPTER 13

NUCLEAR TESTING AND NEW STRATEGIC FRAMEWORKS: THE NEED FOR A STRATEGIC NUCLEAR FRAMEWORK RESPONSIVE TO TERRORIST THREATS

Charles Meade

Before 11 September 2001, RAND examined a range of nuclear postures for the United States under the emerging strategic framework of the new Bush administration. At the time, important issues included the following factors:

- the prospect that the United States would deploy a national missile defence and abrogate the Anti Ballistic Missile (ABM) Treaty;
- the evolving position of the United States on the Comprehensive Nuclear Test Ban Treaty (CTBT) and nuclear testing in general;
- continuing concerns regarding nuclear proliferation;
- changes in the strategic relationships between the United States and Russia and the United States and China, considering the above.

RAND carried out its analysis through a series of "Day After" exercises on the United States policy options regarding the CTBT. The United States Senate had rejected ratification in October 1999, and the new administration was debating whether it would support efforts for the international implementation of the treaty. Policy questions included:

- how the positions of the United States on the CTBT would impact other national security goals;
- whether the complete rejection of CTBT implementation by the United Sates would have a negative impact on relations between the United States and the Russian Federation or the ability to deploy missile defences;

- whether these positions would promote international non-proliferation;
- and most importantly, whether the positions would be robust under a range of plausible political futures.

As part of the exercises, we constructed an emerging strategic nuclear framework illustrating connections between top-level national security goals, nuclear weapons policy, and the details of policy implementation (i.e., diplomatic efforts, nuclear testing activities, research and development programmes). Within this framework, we examined the potential for the policies of the United States to propagate instability across strategic linkages (e.g., policy connections between the CTBT and national missile defence).

For the exercises, we assumed the United States would adopt a "muddle through" policy on the CTBT whereby it would provide only limited support for international implementation, in effect opting neither to block nor promote the treaty. We then considered a range of possible scenarios where the United States posture is tested by unexpected proliferation events and attending international pressures.

From the exercises, we found that a "muddle through" position on the CTBT would create instability in the national security framework, in that the United States policy on nuclear testing was likely to change and there was a possibility of large-scale changes in strategic alliances within Asia. Importantly, the strategy seemed to have limited capability to prevent nuclear proliferation. With this insight, the principal conclusion from the exercise was that a political compromise on the CTBT (i.e., "muddle through") would limit the capacity of the United States to advance a non-proliferation agenda.

This analysis has important implications for the nuclear framework of the United States following 11 September 2001. Specifically it emphasises the mismatch between the current nuclear postures and the political requirement to prevent terrorist attacks. Despite hopes to the contrary, it seems clear that nuclear weapons provide only a minimal deterrent against terrorist attacks. And there are large uncertainties regarding the potential use of nuclear weapons in combat situations. Specifically, would the United States rule out the use of nuclear weapons in responding to a terrorist attack?

We concluded that nuclear stability in the post-11 September environment would require consensus on a number of difficult questions. Specifically,

- what would be the elements of a national security strategy to reduce the threats from terrorist attacks;
- is there a need for a large-scale realignment of current United States priorities (i.e., national missile defence compared to non-proliferation efforts);
- what is the role of the nuclear stockpile of the United States in a world focused on terrorist threats;
- and would the United Sates consider the use of nuclear weapons in the war on terrorism?

While one can imagine a protracted debate on the above questions, we emphasise that there are large risks stemming from an ambiguous policy position. Specifically, maintenance of the current nuclear posture requires substantial expenditures and infrastructure. In a world of limited resources, these investments could constrain the capacity of the United States to respond to new threats. Similarly, there needs to be consensus on the deterrent value of nuclear weapons against terrorist threats. If their contribution is small, there are large risks if decision-makers develop false confidence in the value of their nuclear stockpiles. Finally, a lack of consensus on the use of nuclear weapons could be extremely corrosive to negotiating positions, strategic alliances and decision-making in a wartime setting.